Rafael Bortolini

A tool for sharing learning objects

Rafael Bortolini

A tool for sharing learning objects

Developing a plugin for the Moodle system using PHP and MySQL

ScienciaScripts

Imprint

Cover image: www.ingimage.com

This book is a translation from the original published under ISBN 978-613-9-72632-5.

Publisher:
Sciencia Scripts
is a trademark of
Dodo Books Indian Ocean Ltd. and OmniScriptum S.R.L publishing group

120 High Road, East Finchley, London, N2 9ED, United Kingdom
Str. Armeneasca 28/1, office 1, Chisinau MD-2012, Republic of Moldova, Europe
Printed at: see last page
ISBN: 978-620-7-90161-6

ACKNOWLEDGEMENTS

I would like to dedicate this work to my brother Daniel Bortolini for always supporting me in continuing my studies. Thank you!

A very special thank you to God, my mum Lenir and my dad Osvaldino, because without them I wouldn't have got this far. Thank you!

To Professor Márcia Moraes, PhD, for helping me to write this work. Thank you!

To all those friends and relatives who took part in or contributed to the completion of this course.

Thank you!

SUMMARY

SUMMARY

The aim of this work is to investigate the possibilities of developing a new module for managing learning objects in Moodle *(Modular Object Oriented Dynamic Learning Environment).* Moodle is a tool for managing information related to distance learning courses, which aims to help educators create a virtual learning environment to support activities associated with their pedagogical project. Moodle is used by the community of teachers and students at PUCRS for both undergraduate and postgraduate courses. Teachers who use this environment have observed some restrictions with regard to the set of functionalities available, one of which is the impossibility of sharing materials. The aim of this research project is to see what aspects of the functionalities already available can be expanded through the use of new functionalities, with a view to addressing this restriction related to the use of materials.

CHAPTER 1

INTRODUCTION

According to Wiley (2001), the use of technology can help teachers develop different and innovative methodologies for working with students. The author believes that technology should be at the service of the educational process, expanding possibilities and providing alternatives for students to construct and produce their own knowledge. The author also believes that new technologies integrated into a virtual learning environment make it possible to review and diversify teaching practices.

There are virtual learning environments available that bring together various tools and resources to help educators create and maintain *online* courses. These courses can be semi- or fully distance learning. However, most of these environments are closed packages that do not allow the educator to add new functionalities to them. Building such environments with all the desired functionalities is not a simple task, as it requires advanced computer skills (Olsen, 2002).

The aim of this final project is to develop a *plug-in* for the Moodle virtual learning environment. The purpose of this plug-in is *to* share learning objects with Moodle users in order to reuse and encourage the use of learning objects by teachers and to make the classroom environment more dynamic through the exploration of these objects. A Learning Object (LO) can be defined as a digital resource that can be used, reused and is intended to assist in the learning process in order to develop new knowledge and skills in users. (Tarouco, 2004) As digital resources and usually modular, LOs can be easily adapted for use and reuse in the learning process.

Some examples of Learning Objects are: Simulators, videos, games, tutorials, interactive websites, encyclopaedias, programmes developed in different programming languages and other resources that support learning in some way. As we can use LOs to help and streamline teaching and learning practices, the use of LOs in education should be encouraged by showing them to users who want to use them but don't know about them. In this way, new users benefit and acquire new forms and sources of knowledge and content (Tarouco, 2004).

This document is organised into five chapters. Chapter two describes the theoretical background used to develop the work. Chapter three presents the proposal for a tool for sharing LOs. Chapter four presents the final considerations and future work. Chapter five lists the references used.

CHAPTER 2

THEORETICAL BACKGROUND

According to Keegan (1991), there are different types of education: face-to-face, semi-presential and distance. Face-to-face education is what we've been used to since we were children, where there is a classroom and a teacher teaching content to the class, all of whom are in the same physical space at the same time; semi-presential education is a middle ground between face-to-face and distance learning, where we can have both face-to-face classes in a classroom and classes through technological means, most of which take place through some form of available technology and the percentage of virtual versus face-to-face classes varies greatly. The semi-presential modality is widespread and is gaining more and more followers. "Although this means of teaching may seem new to most people, it has actually been used since the 18th century, it didn't emerge from a vacuum, it has a long history of experimentation, successes and failures."

1.1 Distance Learning

For some time, distance education was almost restricted to the distribution of teaching materials to students and the assessment of programme content by tutors. However, this modality began to be strongly influenced by the appearance of the first personal computers in the 1980s and its significant advance in the 1990s, when its use began to be explored due to the new digital media. Also in the 1990s, the Internet spread rapidly around the world with the arrival of the Web, providing a new form of distance learning, characterised by communication between student and teacher via a computer network. All of this was possible thanks to the emergence and advancement of various development tools for web applications, such as programming languages like *Perl (Practical Extraction and Report Language),* PHP *(Hypertext Preprocessor),* ASP (*Active Server Pages),* JSP (*JavaServer Pages)* and *frameworks* (software development support structures) (Tarouco, 2004).

In the face of Distance Education (DE), the need has arisen for increasingly versatile means that are closer to the reality of students, teachers and administrative staff in distance learning courses. In this context, different software products have been developed in the quest to bring people together in virtual communities through tools that enable the exchange of information, experiences and the generation of new knowledge. These applications are known as virtual learning environments and their use ranges from short online courses to postgraduate courses. By offering specific resources and an environment rich in interaction, virtual learning environments become a concrete basis for online distance learning courses.

A Virtual Learning *Environment* (VLE) is a set of tools for administering courses via a computer network, such as the Internet. In this environment, the teacher can make content available, interact with students and teach them at a distance using multimedia resources or others that enable various forms of communication (Tarouco, 2004).

1.2 Virtual learning environments

Virtual Learning Environments are software designed to support educational activities. They can help teachers and students in their work and promote the integration of different media and resources. Their purpose is to maintain interactions between people and objects of knowledge in an organised and simple way, as well as stimulating the exchange of ideas and the sharing of knowledge by their users. (Tarouco, 2004)

Today there are numerous environments that bring together a range of resources for creating and structuring distance learning courses. This section presents a survey of the most widely used environments today, covering both commercial software such as *First Collaborative Classroom, LearningSpace, WebBoard* and *WebCT,* as well as those developed by universities and research groups, such as *TeamWave,* Atutor, *Aulanet, TelEduc and Eureka.*

First Collaborative Classroom (FCCC) is a product to support computer conferencing, created by

Centrinity (http://www.centrinity.com), which combines the technologies of email and discussion lists. This software allows the conference moderator to organise messages, readings and information within conferences or files. Permissions can be set to determine which groups can read, write and edit documents in conferences. FCCC is completely cross-platform and works on simple hardware that already exists in schools and communities. It doesn't need a full-time administrator, as administration tasks can be assigned to a single person or distributed to other administrators. (FirstClass, 2007)

LearningSpace Forum is a support environment for distance learning developed by *Lotus/IBM,* which allows the creation of courses based on the *Lotus* Notes/Domino *groupware* environment. This environment supports asynchronous activities, enabling collaborative work between teams with multiple levels of communication. *LearningSpace* has a web interface that facilitates student participation in courses and allows instructors to create their own content. Another feature is the ease with which courses can be developed, and no knowledge of programming languages is required. (Porfiro, 2007)

WebBoard is a *web-based* tool that provides communication solutions for a large number of communities. The environment is a resource for communication, information dissemination and community building. Forums can be used as virtual offices, providing information and support to customers or promoting discussion about a new product under development (Porfiro, 2007).

WebCT was developed as a tool that would allow other educators to build sophisticated *web-based* learning environments without the need for a lot of time, resources or technical expertise. It can be characterised as a tool that facilitates the creation of sophisticated web-based educational environments. Its functionalities include the development of course page designs by educators and the provision of a set of educational tools for the student, which can be easily incorporated into a course. It also provides a set of tools to help the teacher with the task of administering a course. The *WebCT* environment can be used to create fully online courses or to publish materials that complement face-to-face courses. All interaction with the environment takes place via the *browser*, including server administration, course creation, student access and teacher access. (WebCT, 2000)

TeamWave Workplace is designed to support virtual communities and help them grow and prosper. Virtual community members access their communities directly or via the central portal. The software uses a client-server solution to provide permanently accessible locations where people can come together to work and form communities. Using the metaphor of a "Room", *TeamWave Workplace* allows the creation and manipulation of virtual community spaces. Each space or room can fulfil a range of needs, from libraries to archives. The creators of *TeamWave Workplace* claim that this environment can help educators use the Internet to establish a more collaborative learning model, where students can actively interact with the course material, their instructor and other students. They consider this environment to be the "perfect" forum for educational collaboration (Porfiro, 2007).

AulaNet is a co-operative learning environment based on the *WEB,* the project for which began in 1997. Developed at the Software Engineering Laboratory of the Computer Science Department of the Pontifical Catholic University of Rio de Janeiro (PUC-Rio), its aim is to create and support distance learning courses. AulaNet is currently available in Portuguese and English, and its Spanish version is under development. According to its creators, the environment was built using a co-operative approach to web-based instruction, seeking to migrate towards a "dynamic learning community" model. (AulaNet, 2007)

ATutor, according to CNEAD (2009), is a web-based, *open* source Learning and Content Management System (LMS), with the project focussed on an accessible and adaptable environment. Administrators can install or update ATutor in a matter of minutes, developing customised *templates* to give ATutor a fresh look. Educators can quickly assemble and distribute web-based instructional content and easily retrieve and import pre-formatted content to conduct their online courses. Students learn in an adaptable and flexible learning environment.

TelEduc was developed by a team of researchers from NIED, Unicamp's Centre for Informatics Applied to Education. Its main objective was to train teachers in the area of information technology in education. From 1997 to the present day, its tools have been reformulated several times, according to the needs and observations that have arisen. *TelEduc is made* up of three groups of tools: the coordination tools, which aim to organise and support the actions of the course in some way; the administration tools, which aim to support the trainer in managing the course; and the communication tools, which, as the name suggests, aim to establish communication between the participants, enabling them to have a wide visibility of the work carried out. (Porfiro, 2007)

Eureka is an institutional learning environment developed by the Pontifical Catholic University of Paraná (PUC-PR). Its construction process took place in partnership with a communications company, and the development period spanned the years 1998 to 2001. Since its launch, *Eureka* has been constantly restructured, both in terms of its interface and the inclusion of new tools. These redesigns are mainly due to the way in which *Eureka* came about, because with the partnership realised in a business context, the focus of the environment was on corporate education. However, after the project was completed, *Eureka's* scope was remodelled as a resource for promoting academic learning, which consolidated the institutionalisation of the environment, whose tools were revised based on the concept of collaborative learning (EUREKA, 2007).

In addition to the virtual learning environments described above, there is the Moodle environment.

1.2.1 Moodle

Moodle is an open source LMS that is distributed free of charge. It was first devised in the 1990s by Martin Dougiamas when he was *webmaster* at *Curtin University of Technology* in Australia and responsible for administering the LMS used by the university at the time.

The Moodle project led by Martin was born out of the principle of helping those who want to make good use of the Internet to mediate education. To do this, the project combines knowledge from education, specifically the epistemology of constructivism, and the recent methodology of software development, which promotes the construction of knowledge in a collaborative way. Thus, it can be said that the form of development adopted for Moodle is the Bazaar methodology of software production (Raymond, 1999). This development methodology is similar to the one used to create the Linux *kernel,* which explains its constant evolution and the success of this project. Moodle's many advantages from a technological point of view include: (Moodle, 2009)

1. Execution in any operating environment with a *web* server installed and support for the PHP3 language, such as: *Unix, Linux, Windows,* etc.
2. The data is stored in the *MySQL* or *PostgreSQL database,* but another database management system such as *Oracle, Access,* Interbase, etc. can be used;
3. Translation into more than 50 languages, including Spanish, Portuguese, Italian, Japanese, German, etc;
4. Excellent documentation;
5. Strong support for administration and security;
6. Support for IMS standards (this standard will be explained in section 2.3.2.1) In addition to managing a hierarchical database, IMS also manages online transactions and SCORM (XML-based framework, standard defined for distance learning systems), the Scorm standard will be explained in more detail in section 2.3.2.2.

The development of Moodle brings together researchers from various fields: educators, system administrators, instructional designers and programmers. Moodle users and developers maintain a *web* portal, which acts as a centre for information, exchange of experiences, discussion and collaboration among its members. This "moodle.org" portal is an important feature of the Moodle project and a driving force behind its success. All these factors have contributed to several institutions deciding to adopt the Moodle teaching platform. Of the environments described above, Moodle has the most advantages, differentiating it from its main competitors. Moodle has a wide range of educational resources, extremely robust and agile development, and high flexibility in terms of configuration and use. In addition, its extremely modular development makes it easy to add new features that can better adapt Moodle to the needs of the institution using it.

2.2.1.1 Moodle Environment functionalities

The version used for this final project was version 1.9. In the research carried out, the Moodle environment's code and functionalities were analysed. Moodle has an open source code and is available for download at the following address: http://download.moodle.org/.

According to Moodle (2009), the tool offers various functionalities, among which we can highlight:

- **Forums** - Forums are discussion tools through which users can exchange ideas and discuss issues in the course they are taking. They are extremely important because they establish direct contact between users.
- ***Chats*** - Although Moodle is an asynchronous tool, it provides a *Chat function* for its users to communicate synchronously, i.e. in real time.
- **Quizzes** - In this module, the teacher provides questions for the students to answer and demonstrate the knowledge they have acquired during the course. The teacher just needs to build a database of questions and answers.
- **Assignments** - The assignments area allows teachers to grade assignments and also make comments on materials submitted by students. Students can see their grades and the teacher can export the results to Excel.
- ***Wikis - The*** idea of the well-known Wikipedia is available here, allowing several users to build the same page of text in the tool, using a specific language, similar to HTML.
- **Glossaries** - Allows dictionaries of useful terms to be created for course members. In this feature, the user can include texts as well as links to websites and images.
- **Lessons** - This is an assessment, consisting of a number of pages or slides that may have questions interspersed with grading, where continuity depends on the student's performance.
- ***Books*** - These are text-based references that can be created to support students.
- **Sending *emails*** - Allows you to send emails to your users.

In addition to the features mentioned above, several others are available on Moodle's own website (http://www.moodle.org). Moodle uses a *workflow* to manage different levels of system utilisation. This hierarchy is described in Porfiro (2007). There are basically four roles within the tool. They are:

- **Administrator** - Responsible for configuring the tool and making modules available. They manage the entire tool and have exclusive rights, such as removing pages.
- **Teacher** - You can use the pages assigned to you and also appoint other teachers to help you manage the class.
- **Student** - This only uses the functionalities available to the class.
- **Visitor** - The visitor can be a student, this permission is set when creating or editing a course. Those responsible define whether or not a visitor can access a course.

Figure 2.2.1.1 shows the actions that can be carried out by the administrator, teacher and student roles.

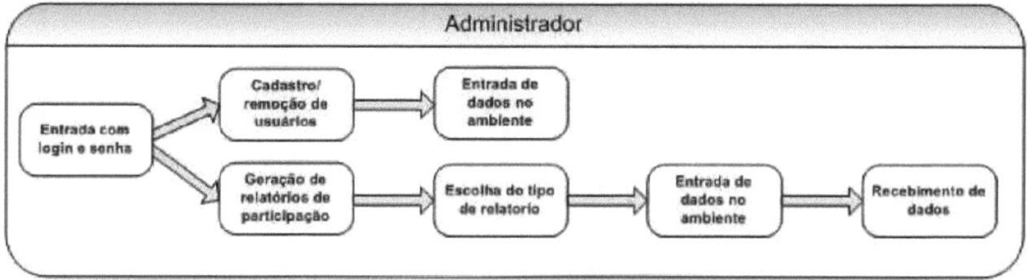

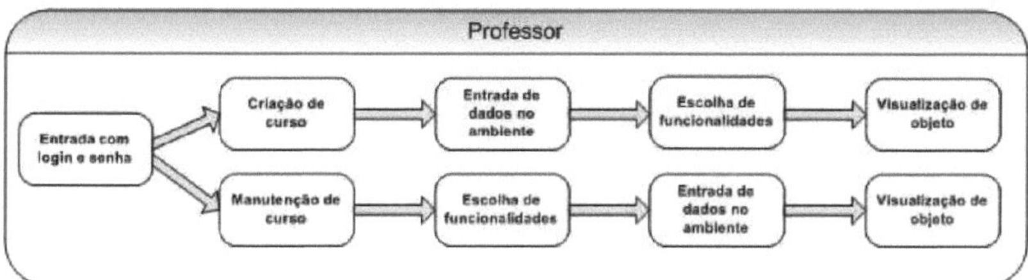

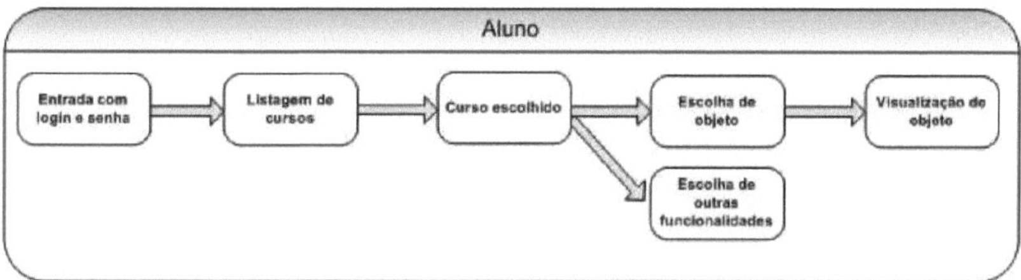

Figure 2.2.1.1

Flow available to Moodle users

(Porfiro, 2007)

2.2.1.2 Methodology for development in the Moodle environment

According to Moodle (2009), Moodle was initially developed on Linux using Apache, Mysql and PHP, but has also been tested with Postgresql and Windows XP, Mac OS X, and NetWare 6.

The requirements for installing Moodle are:

- A web server, with Apache being recommended, but you can use any that supports PHP, such as IIS included in the Windows platform.
- PHP language (version 4.1.0 or higher). PHP 5 is supported from Moodle version 1.4 onwards.

For the database, it is recommended that you use Mysql or Postgresql, as they are fully supported by Moodle. For more information on installing the Moodle environment and the Apache server, see the tutorial in Appendix A.

Moodle has a standard structure defined for files and directories, as described below.

Archives:

- **config.php** - Contains the basic settings. This file does not come with Moodle, it is created automatically from the data provided during installation;

- **install.php** - You must run this script to create config.php;
- **version.php** - Defines the current version of the Moodle code;
- **index.php** - Environment home page.

Directories:

- **admin/** - Codes for administering the service
- **auth/** - User authentication codes;
- **blocks/** - Side **block** codes;
- **calendar/** - Codes for calendar management and presentation;
- **course/** - Codes for displaying and managing courses;
- **doc/** - Moodle help documentation;
- **files/** - Codes for displaying and managing file *uploads;*
- **lang/** - Texts in different languages, one directory per language;
- **lib/** - Moodle core code libraries;
- **login/** - Codes for handling *login and* creating accounts;
- **mod/** - All the main modules added to Moodle;
- **pix/** - Generic site graphics;
- **theme/** - **Theme** packages to change the appearance of the site;
- **user/** - Codes for displaying and managing users.

To develop a module for Moodle there are steps and rules that need to be respected so that the application recognises that group of files as a module. Thus, a module must respect the following rules: (Porfiro, 2007)

1. All the files that make up the module must be in a directory with a name that does not contain numbers or special characters and must be a single word without spaces. This directory should be located in Moodle's /mod folder.
2. All code files must have the .php extension
3. All template files must have the .html extension
4. All access to the database must be done using the functions in the datalib.php file in the Moodle /lib folder.
5. All texts must be handled using Moodle's predefined functions *(get_string()* and *print_string())*. This means that part of the code has to be *standardised to* make it easier to translate the text into other languages. These functions search for keywords in the language file located in the module's /lang directory. This file must have the name of the module followed by the .php extension.
6. The name of the module is defined in the language file by assigning the desired name to the modulename variable. To define the plural, the plural name must be assigned to the modulenames variable.
7. Each code file must include the Moodle config.php file *require_once("../../*config.php"); necessary for user identification via require_login() and isadmin(), isteacherQ, iscreatorf) or isstudent().
8. All help files should be translatable by placing new help files in the appropriate directory. E.g. lang/en/help
9. All texts within Moodle, especially those coming from users, should be printed using the format_text() function. This ensures that the text is filtered and properly cleaned. In addition, the following files are mandatory:
    - **mod.html** - An initial form that will be displayed in Moodle, used to create and modify the *plugin.*
    - **version.php** - Indicates the version of the module and is useful for later upgrades. It should

also indicate the time interval at which moodle's cron.php script updates the data relating to the module.

- **icon.gif**- Small representative image of the module
- **index.php** - Page listing all existing instances of the module
- **view.php** - Page that allows you to view a particular instance
- **lib.php** - This file should contain the following functions, which must be implemented in order to create the *plugin.*
  - **modulo_add_instance()** - Code to add a new instance
  - **modulo_update_instance()** - Code to update an instance
  - **modulo_delete_instance()** - Code to delete an instance
  - **modulo_user_outline()** - Code that lists summaries about the user
  - **modulo_user_complete()** - Code that provides all the user information

If the module needs to use a database, there should be a db/ directory within the module directory with a mysql.php and/or postgres.php file and also a mysql.sql and/or postgres.sql file depending on the database management system on which the Moodle application is running. The php file is used to make updates to the database in the event that a previous version of the same module is already installed on the system. The sql file consists of the SQL statements that will create the tables in the database that the module will use. All tables must start with the name prefix_ followed by a name. The prefix value is then assigned by Moodle when the SQL code is executed.

The main table must have the same name as the module (e.g. prefix_module_name) and must contain at least the following fields:

- **id** - INT10 auto incremental as primary index
- **course** - With the id of the course to which the instance belongs
- **name** - The full name of each instance of the module

The other tables must be named following the **prefix_module_name** rule (Moodle, 2009). Once all these steps have been completed, the implementation of a new module can begin.

2.3 Learning Objects

A Learning Object is defined as an entity, digital or non-digital, that can be used, re-used or referenced during technology supported learning. Examples of technology-supported learning include computer-based training systems, interactive learning environments, computer-aided instructional systems, distance learning systems and collaborative learning environments. Examples of Learning Objects include multimedia content, instructional content, teaching objectives, instructional software and software in general and people, organisations or events referenced during technology-supported teaching. (Balbino, 2007)

LOs are based on the object-oriented paradigm, allowing them to be reused in an easier and more organised way. The basic idea is that the objects are like blocks with which the learning context will be built (Tarouco, 2004).

A learning object can be used in different contexts and in different virtual learning environments. To fulfil this characteristic, each object has its visual part, which interacts with the user, separated from the content and instructional data of the object. The main characteristic of learning objects is their reusability, which is put into practice through repositories, which store objects logically, allowing them to be located by searching for themes, by level of difficulty, by author or by relationship with other objects. In English-speaking countries, a vast number of repositories are available, used and reused in a variety of contexts (Wiley, 2001).

Another definition comes from Muzio (2001), who uses the term learning object as a granular, reusable piece of information that is independent of media and the term communication object for instructional purposes. According to this author, learning objects can be defined as communication objects used for instructional purposes, ranging from maps and graphs to video demonstrations and interactive simulations.

The learning object can be divided into three distinct parts: the objective, where the learner searches for the information that their learning object will intervene with, the institutional content, where the tools for creating a learning object will be provided, and the practice, or *feedback,* which is when the learner will carry out the necessary tests on the learning object to check that the object has met the expectations proposed in the first part of the project, and if it has, the learner will be able to return to their object and update it whenever they need to.

According to Wiley (2001) some characteristics common to all learning objects are:

- Portability - A learning object must be able to be "transported" to different platforms.
- Re-use - A learning object should be able to be used in several courses.
- Modularity - A learning object is always part of a complete course and can contain other learning objects or be contained in one or more objects or in one or more courses.
- Metadata - This is a complete description of the learning object, its content and its use. This is an important item because it allows the object to be catalogued and coded, making it understandable for different platforms. The two main existing *metadata* specifications are the IEEE's LOM *(Learning Object Metadata)* and the IMS, which points to the use of the XML language as the standard for metadata schematisation. Both specifications are compatible and complementary and have become standard in distance education.

Issues such as large-scale production, reduced production time, lower costs and reuse, as well as better organisation of the creation process, are relevant and justify the implementation and use of learning objects. Wiley (2001) also suggests that learning objects, being digital units and available on the Internet, can be created collaboratively and accessed simultaneously from a repository, and new versions can be obtained immediately.

2.3.1 Metadata

According to Bertoletti-De-Marchi (2004), metadata, or data about data, works in a similar way to a library catalogue. It provides information about a particular resource, promoting interoperability, identification, sharing, integration, use, reuse, management and retrieval in a more efficient way. They are descriptive data that can provide information on the title, author, date, publication, keywords, description, location of the resource, among others. They can be compared to a labelling system that describes the resource, its objectives and characteristics, showing how, when and by whom the resource was stored, and how it is formatted. Metadata is essential for understanding the stored resource, it describes semantic information about the resource.

The use of standards in collection documentation makes the exchange of data between institutions using the same standard easier, allowing data to be shared. Many standards around the world are being developed for this purpose

In the educational field, metadata is used to describe learning objects, i.e. instructional resources that can be reused by different environments, allowing them to be presented and quickly retrieved according to the needs of the educational context being worked on. The purpose of these standards is not only to facilitate the sharing and exchange of objects, but also to enable the development of catalogues and inventions while taking into account the diversity of cultures and languages in which learning objects and their metadata will be exploited (IEEE, 2002).

In this work, three learning object metadata standards were studied: IMS, SCORM and LOM, which will be explained in the following sections. Both metadata standards fulfil their objectives because:

- They outline the units of information that need to be recorded in order to document a collection correctly (they structure data or metadata standards);
- Promote a format and conventions for storing information

- (data content or standards);
- Suggest terminology sources (evaluate data or vocabulary standards). (IEEE, 2002)

2.3.2 Standard for Learning Objects

To facilitate the common adoption of the learning objects proposal, the LTSC *(Learning Technology Standards Committee)* of the IEEE *(Institute of Electrical and Electronics Engineers)* was formed in 1996 to develop and provide standards for instructional technology. Without such standards, universities, corporations and other organisations around the world would have no way of ensuring the interoperability of their instructional technologies, specifically their learning objects. Meta data standards for learning objects cover the minimum set of attributes needed to allow these objects to be managed, localised and assessed (Balbino, 2007).

2.3.2.1 IMS standard

Over the last few years, academic, governmental and commercial organisations, as well as industry consortia, have been developing specifications and establishing relationships between available educational content in order to enable the interoperability of educational products. Among the groups dedicated to this issue is the *MCC (Aviation Industry CBT Committee),* whose aim is to define how data exchange between content management systems and generic educational applications should be carried out. This involves defining a format for exchanging content and its entire structure between systems produced by different manufacturers. Like the AICC, one of the aims of the IMS group's specification is to define the attributes needed to describe educational resources available on the Internet. These initiatives are joined by the W3C. (W3C, 2000)

All the initiatives are aimed at defining a methodology, specification or standard for the exchange of educational content. For the specification of the characteristics of educational content, the IMS standard was based on the analogy made with the system used in libraries. Searching in a library or bookshop begins by identifying a characteristic of the book you want. The multiple categories of the card system (e.g. author, title, subject) provide different ways of finding the same book.

Just like books in a library, materials available on the Web also need a similar form of meta-information, which enables users to describe their documents in a way that makes it easier for others to use, locate, evaluate, access and manipulate the resources available online. This meta-information that describes a book or content available on the Web is made up of attributes of this content. In this case, the educational resource is the data, and the set of attributes that describe it is the meta-information. Examples of meta-information for educational materials are title, author, educational level and objective of the material.

Behind the creation of meta-information is the need for more efficient search mechanisms. People who are looking for a material or resource will use metadata to describe the types of resources they want and people who will provide these resources will make the material available with meta-information in order to make their resources accessible to interested users. This model is designed to provide an infrastructure to support meta-information using XML *(eXtensible Markup Language),* forming a meta-information community through many web-based activities. XML is a simple and very flexible markup language. This language makes it possible to exchange information on the Web, as it defines the formatting of HTML pages and the description of resources. Its simple syntax can be used to support the definition of Web server content, in the use of e-commerce, enabling the rapid exchange of information on the Web, through electronic bookshops to locate titles or volumes (IMS, 2005).

2.3.2.2 SCORM standard

The *Sharable Content Object Reference Model* (SCORM) is a reference model for learning objects. SCORM is a unified set of recommendations for developing and visualising educational content via the Web. This set of specifications defines a content aggregation model, a sequencing model and an execution environment for *web-based* learning objects (Tarouco, 2004).

One of the aims of SCORM is to make it possible for different Virtual Learning Environments - VLEs (such as Moodle) to run and monitor content and activities developed by authoring tools from different suppliers, which means independence from the hardware and software platform on which the content will be created and used. Another feature is the reusability of content and even entire courses in different VLEs, through the migration of courses that are packaged using the SCORM specifications with little effort. In the specific case of Moodle, it is possible to include SCORM Activities, which can range from small Learning Objects - such as the exercises included in this course - to the content of entire courses. (SCORM, 2008)

One of the great advantages of using SCORM to develop content for distance education is its focus on reusability, accessibility, interoperability and durability. In addition, content developed in accordance with SCORM is context-independent, i.e. it will work in a variety of situations, whether inserted into a learning management environment or as part of an online course published directly on the *Web* (Tarouco, 2004).

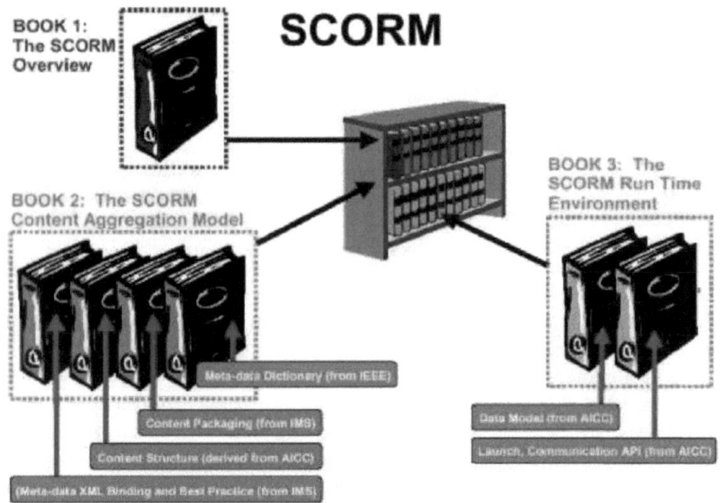

Figure 2.3.1

SCORM as a set of specifications (Porfiro, 2007).

The SCORM standard defines a model of "how to make" and "how to run" *web-based* courses. The standard's norms are a collection of specifications, creating a comprehensive and appropriate set of web-based learning skills that enable interoperability, accessibility and content reuse.

SCORM allows the creation of small learning objects, which are called SCO's *(Shareable Content Objects)* and can be used together to create a learning path for the student to follow during the course, while also being able to track the student's progress.

The main advantages of using the SCORM standard are:

- **Standardisation:** in the way objects relate to the systems that support them;
- **Re-utilisation of SCO's:** allows these objects to be used in different

contexts, i.e. the same content can be used in different disciplines and modules;

- **Flexibility of learning:** makes it possible for students to create different learning paths;
- **Portability or migration:** allows objects to be independent of the learning platform.

According to Morais (2008) "this standard also describes methods for conducting communications between the course and the learning management environment. This is referred to as the SCORM execution environment, which includes communications about the status of the course, i.e. what materials are being presented to the student, as well as information about the student's progress during the course."

These facilities provided by SCORM have made it a standard in the development of learning objects.

2.3.2.3 LOM *(Learning Object Metadata)*

The aim of the IEEE-LTSC consortium was to create a *semantic structure* that would make it possible to *catalogue learning* materials, guaranteeing their efficient identification, reuse, management, interoperability, sharing, integration and retrieval. These cataloguing/indexing rules, or *metadata,* resulted in the IEEE-LOM International *Learning Object Metadata* specification, finalised in 2002.

In practice, the IEEE-LOM functions as a *header* that provides information about the learning object linked to it (if it is a digital component) or referenced by it (if it is a non-digital component, such as books, documents, videos, places, people and events). This means that it *does not interfere with* the content or objectives of the learning object, *nor does it define* rules to be followed in its construction. Its function is to group together useful data in one place in a standardised format that can be understood by humans and (some of them) by machines (Balbino, 2007).

The LOM suggests a schema that defines a data hierarchy for LO metadata. At the top of the hierarchy are nine categories: (IEEE, 2002)

- General: general information about the object as a whole, includes information such as: identification number, title, abstract, keywords;
- Lifestyle: characteristics related to the history and current state of the OA, with information such as creation date, authors and versions;
- Meta-Metadata: information about its own metadata instances;
- Technical: technical requirements and technical characteristics of the LOs, it contains information such as: file format, resources needed for its execution;
- Educational: pedagogical and educational characteristics of OAs, it contains information such as: objectives and type of mediation;
- Rights: information related to copyright, includes information such as copying and distribution rules;
- Relation: defines the relationship between learning objects;
- Annotation: category related to object-related comments;
- Classification: describes the Object in relation to the classification system.

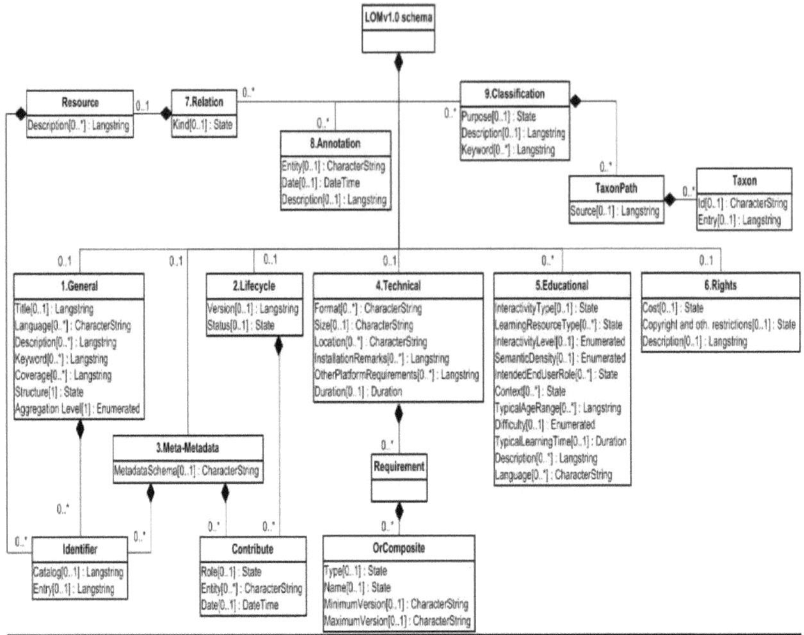

Figure 2.3.2

LOM base schema (BOHL, 2002).

Despite the wide range of information (the vast majority of which is optional), it is relatively easy to submit existing materials to the standard, since there is no need to change their internal structure. By dealing only with the indexing of teaching materials, without worrying about their content and objectives, IEEE-LTSC circumvents the very technical limitations imposed by the definition drafted in 1998. Such flexibility has allowed it to be widely used by the *e-learning* market in various standardisation initiatives, such as ADL/SCORM certification. (Balbino, 2007)

LOM is used in more modern and comprehensive standards such as SCORM. (BOHL, 2002).

In addition to metadata, all the content of a LO needs to be stored and structured so that the textual content, its scenes and images can be represented, identified and manipulated quickly and easily. In this respect, again, each team adopts a different structure or representation model, making the process of reuse (and even maintenance) difficult, especially when using a LO repository. It is therefore necessary to analyse the different architectures of existing LOs in order to make their information structure more comprehensive and standardise it. The prototype used a combination of some LOM categories, since according to Balbino (2007) it is not compulsory to implement all the categories in order to submit the material to the LOM standard.

2.3.3 Learning object repository

A LO repository can be defined as a place, a kind of database, usually integrated into a learning system, in which LOs are organised and stored in order to make them easier to find, whether for use or reuse, and to facilitate the reuse of learning objects in order to make them suitable for the user's needs. Repositories store the objects themselves, as well as meta-data (information about the objects) about the stored objects. Through these repositories, it is possible to locate, add and obtain the objects for use in different forms of teaching. The repository of educational objects can be local (a single institution) or distributed (a consortium of institutions). There are currently several consortia of academic institutions organising repositories of educational objects. One of the most relevant efforts is the *Advanced Distributed Learning* (ADL) initiative sponsored by the *Office of the Secretary of Defense* (OSD), which is a joint effort by the US government, industry and academia to establish a new educational context that allows the interoperability of learning tools and content on a global scale. (ADL, 2003)

The description of the cataloguing attributes of the objects (metadata) should allow them to be searched and retrieved using different criteria. Learning support tools can interact directly with the repository, selecting and retrieving objects and combining them to form learning support units that meet the individual needs of each student. (Souza, 2005)

2.3.3.1 Main repositories of learning objects

LOs are usually stored in places where they are organised in order to facilitate access to them. Through these sites, it is possible to locate, add and retrieve LOs. Repositories allow you to search efficiently and more accurately. The number of object repositories has been growing rapidly over the last few years:

CAREO (htt://www.careo.org) and MERLOT (http://www.merlot.org) - These are learning object repositories located at the University of Alberta, Canada and California State University, USA, respectively. They allow you to search for and include digital material in any format. As in the previous example, the material does not necessarily have to have been conceived as a learning object (in fact, not even as educational material). When registering a new item, the user needs to fill in a form which is the object's metadata.

RIVED (Virtual Interactive Education Network): It is a repository that aims to produce digital pedagogical content, in the form of OA, that can help develop students' reasoning and critical thinking. The content produced by RIVED is public and can be accessed via a search engine, which allows you to view, copy and comment on published content (Rosa, 2008).

CLOE *(Co-Operative Learnware Object Exchange)* is another learning object repository developed at the University of Waterloo in Canada, which allows not only the storage but also the collaborative development of learning objects and their relationship with other objects in the database. Access to the repository is restricted to some Canadian universities (Rosa, 2008).

CESTA (Collection of Entities Supporting the Use of Technology in Learning): Developed by the Federal University of Rio Grande do Sul (UFRGS), with the aim of organising the register of objects that are developed at the university (Porto, 2003).

LabVirt (Virtual Laboratory of the University of São Paulo (USP)): Another example of a Brazilian OA repository, LabVirt has a large number of objects from disciplines such as Physics and Chemistry (Porto, 2003).

CESTA *(Repository ofObjects with Semantic Access for E-learning)*\ Developed by the IME - Military Institute of Engineering, Rio de Janeiro - this is a repository designed to help education professionals find the content available in the system. The system stores learning objects - content, plus characteristics and properties (metadata) - as well as a set of associations (or predicates) that show the relationships that a learning object has with other learning objects (Lopes, 2004).

2.4 PHP language

Moodle is entirely developed using the PHP language *(Hypertext Preprocessor,* but originally it stood for *Personal Home Page).* PHP is an easy language to learn, as it allows you to connect directly to a large number of relational databases, while others need drivers to perform the same task. PHP is completely free and open source and can be downloaded from the official website, http://www.php.net.

PHP was originally created by Rasmus Lerdorf in mid-1994 and written in Perl, being rewritten for C to include database access. As this tool spread throughout the virtual world, Rasmus provided some documentation for the software and officially named it PHP v.1.0. With its increasing use, more and more features were added, making the language more and more powerful. At this time, other programmers joined Rasmus, helping to improve the language. PHP is now in version 5, where one of its current features is object orientation.

Main features of the PHP language:

- **Open** source - the entire PHP source code is available;
    - **Zero cost** - it's free. It can be purchased on the official website:
- **Multiplatform** - you can run on *Unix, Linux, Windows and* ECT platforms;

In addition, we can mention the ability to read information from the XML standard, file processing (reading, writing, both in text and binary format), the manipulation of complex variables, the use of functions and classes and the generation of *"Java Script"* code, or any other for client-side processing, the manipulation of e-mails, document management.

The interaction between PHP, the WEB server and the user's *browser* is shown in the figure below:

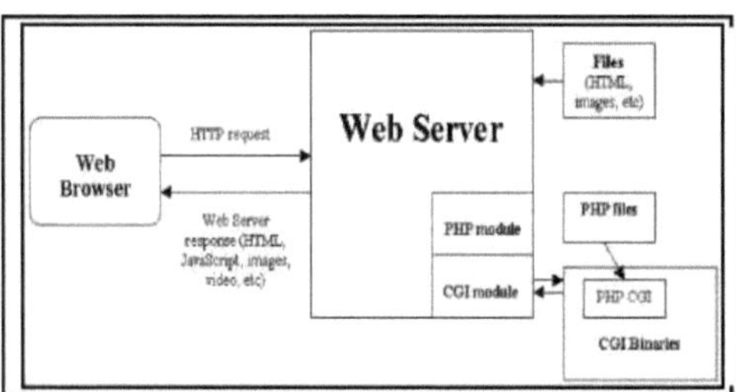

Figure 2.4

Interaction between PHP/Web Server/Browser (Porfiro, 2007).

CHAPTER 3

OAS SHARING TOOL

Given the advantages of using LOs described in section 2.3, the general aim of this work is to develop a *plug-in* for the Moodle virtual teaching environment. This *plug-in makes* it possible for teachers to register and share learning objects (LOs). Considering that the teaching materials used by teachers in their Moodle courses are not learning objects (LOs) in the conceptual sense of the word, as they do not have related metadata, we believe that Moodle can be a great LO repository as long as teachers can transform their materials into LOs. As well as making it possible to include LOs in Moodle, currently only the teacher who has registered the material can use it and include it in their virtual classroom, the idea of this prototype is to allow not only the author to have access to the LO, but to allow more teachers to include it in their classrooms, reducing the redundancy of material and making it possible to reuse it.

In order to make it possible to transform materials into LOs and share these LOs, the teacher will have a series of functionalities at their disposal, such as: registering metadata, registering learning objects, associating metadata with a learning object, making objects available for use by other teachers and reusing objects registered by other teachers and made available by the same teacher to other teachers.

In order to reuse a learning object, it is necessary to query the repository using a set of metadata as a resource. After selecting the metadata to be used in the search, the teacher will get back a list of learning objects that have been made public for inclusion in their virtual classrooms. In this way, only those materials that have been made learning objects through metadata registration can be retrieved from the Moodle database as possible learning objects to be reused.

The LOM standard (presented in section 2.3.2.3) was chosen to implement the tool due to its widespread use. Below are the fields that were used from some of the categories available in LOM:

From the "General" category, the following fields were used to describe the metadata: "identification number (ID)", "title", "keywords", "summary".

From the "Lifestyle" category, the following fields were used: "author" and "creation date".

From the "Technical" category, the "file format" field was used; this last field is filled in automatically when a new learning object is registered.

The "Rights" category suggests information on rules for distributing materials. This category will not be implemented as it is considered to be outside the context of the work. It is assumed that the materials will only be registered by teachers if they have no legal impediment to copying and distributing them to other teachers.

If the metadata described above does not fulfil the user's requirements, it can be modified and/or added depending on the usage needs. These modifications are only possible by modifying the existing code of the new module. For more information on how to modify or add new metadata, see "Appendix B" available at the end of this document.

In the following sections, the tool's functionalities will be detailed in the use case diagrams in section 3.1, the ER diagram in section 3.2 and the prototype structure specification in section 3.3. Section 3.4 presents an example of using the tool and section 3.5 describes the usability evaluation carried out using the Ergolist software.

3.1 Definition of use cases

The modelling of the tool, containing the identified use cases, is presented below. Figure 3.1 shows the functionalities that will be added to the Moodle environment.

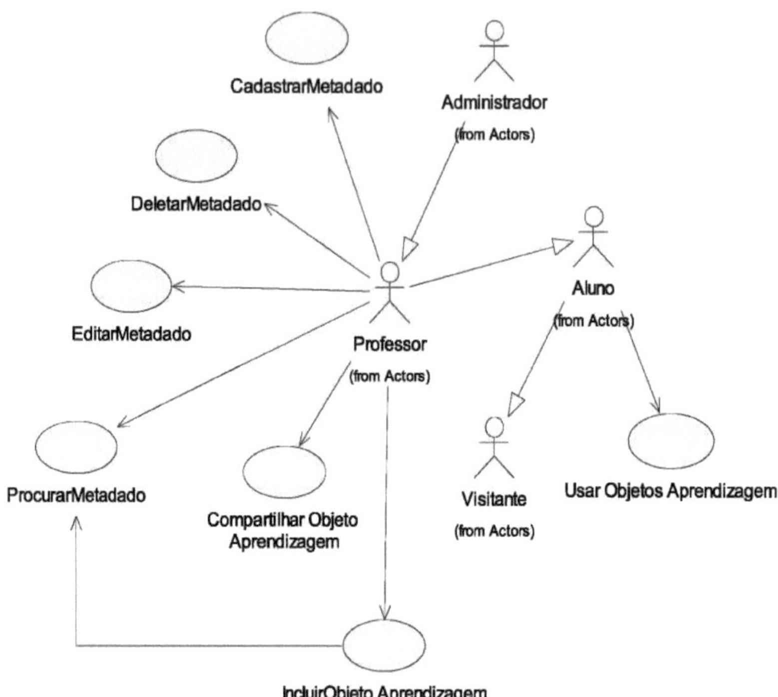

Figure 3.1 *Use cases - FUNCTIONALITIES THAT WILL BE ADDED TO MOODLE.*

UC- 01 REGISTER METADATA

Preconditions:

- User is logged in to Moodle as a Teacher or Administrator.

Actor	System
1. Administrator/Teacher clicks on "Edit_OA" available in the new block.	
	2. 0 system shows a screen with the following items: A table with the metadata already registered by it, above this table there is a button with the option "New Learning Object".
3. Administrator/Teacher clicks on the "New Learning Object" button.	
	4. The system displays a form with fields (title, summary, keywords, difficulty, language and learning object).
5. The teacher provides the data and clicks the "Send data" button.	
	6. The system validates the data and registers the new learning object.

UC- 02 EDIT METADATA

Preconditions:

- The user must be logged into Moodle as a Teacher or Administrator and have at least one metadata registered.

Actor	System
1. Administrator/Teacher clicks on "Edit_OA" available in the new block	
	2. 0 system shows a screen with the following items: A table with the metadata already registered by it, in this table there is a column with the option to "edit" the metadata.
3. Administrator/Teacher clicks on the "edit" link.	
	4. The system displays a form with fields (title, summary, keywords, language, difficulty).
5. Teacher provides data and	
click on the "Send data" button.	
	6. System validates the data and edits the metadata.

UC- 03 DELETE METADATA

Preconditions:

- The user must be logged into Moodle as a Teacher or Administrator and have at least one metadata registered.

Actor	System
1. Administrator/Teacher clicks on "Edit_OA" available in the new block.	
	2. 0 system shows a screen with the following items: A table with the metadata already registered by it, in this table there is a column with the option to "delete" the metadata.
3. Administrator/Teacher clicks on the "delete" link.	
	4.0 The system displays an alert to confirm the deletion of the metadata.
5. Administrator/Teacher confirms deletion.	
	5. The system deletes the metadata and the corresponding learning object.

UC- 04 SHARING LEARNING OBJECTS

Preconditions:

- User is logged in to Moodle as a Teacher or Administrator.
- Have at least one learning object registered.

Actor	System
1 Administrator/Teacher clicks on "Files" available in the	

"Administration" menu.	
	2. The system displays a screen with the following items: A table with all the files (learning objects) registered in the system and a column with the option to share the metadata.
3. Teacher/Administrator clicks on the "share" link corresponding to the line in the file.	
	4.0 The system shows a metadata registration form with the following fields (title, summary and
	keywords, difficulty, language), the learning object is already automatically populated with the previously selected file.
5. The teacher provides the data and clicks the "send data" button.	
	6. The system validates the data and registers the new metadata.

UC- 05 SEARCH FOR LEARNING OBJECTS

Preconditions:

- User is logged in to Moodle as a Teacher or Administrator.
- Have at least one learning object registered.

Actor	System
1. Administrator/Teacher clicks on "Search_OA" available in the new block	
	2. The system displays a screen with the following items: A table with the objects registered by all the teachers. Above this table is a text field and a menu with the extensions of the files already registered.
3. Administrator/Teacher types in a (keyword or part of it) and/or selects an extension.	
	4. The system performs a search based on the search data and assembles a new table with the data returned after the search.

UC- 06 INCLUDE LEARNING OBJECT

Preconditions:

- User is logged in to Moodle as a Teacher or Administrator.
- Have at least one learning object registered.
- Includes UC-05.

5. Administrator/Teacher selects one or more learning objects by clicking on the "checkbox" next to the file and then selecting the "include file" option available in the menu just below the table.	
	6. The system displays a new screen with a message informing you that the file(s) have been successfully included. Just below the message is a link with the option to return to the previous screen.

3.2 Defining the ER diagram

The figure below shows the tables that will be added to the Moodle database, defined for the prototype.

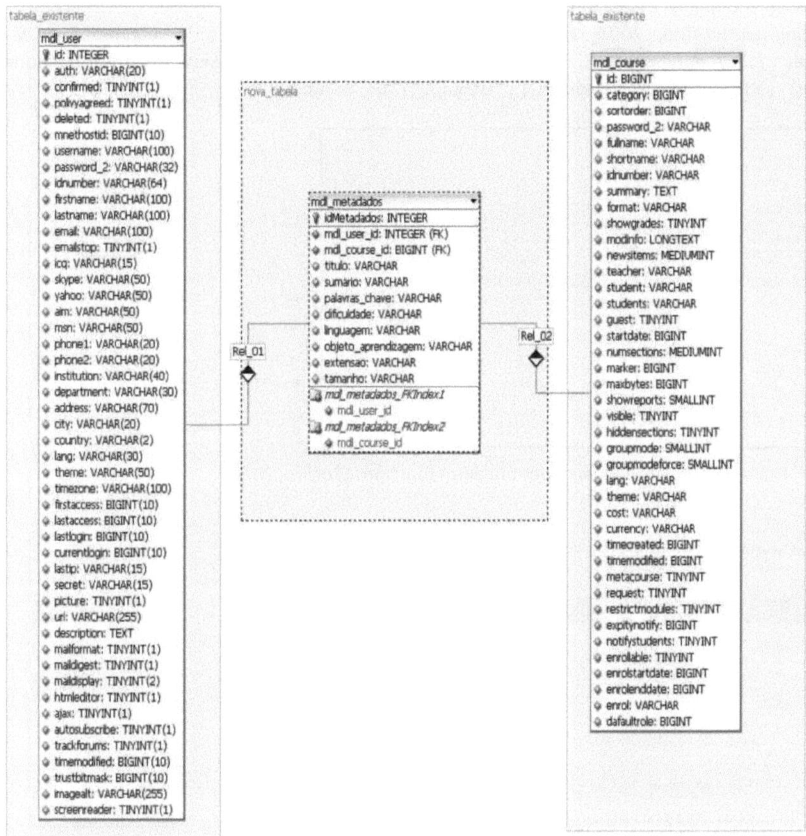

Figure 3.2
ER diagram

The "mdl_metadata" table keeps records of the metadata and learning objects registered in the Moodle environment. The fields used for registration are: id of the metadata, id of the teacher who registered the metadata, id of the course where the metadata was registered, title, summary, keywords, difficulty, language and the physical path of the learning object called "learning_object" as well as the extension and physical size of the file.

3.3 Developing the tool

The files and how they were implemented will be presented below, the tools used and how to install them will be explained in Appendix A, available at the end of this document.

3.3.1 Prototype structure

The development of the prototype was based on the "index.php" file in the "files" folder at the root of Moodle. This file was used as a base because it contains a lot of code related to "files". Some parts of these codes were utilised and the necessary functionalities added to the new module.

According to (Porfiro, 2007) each code file must include moodle's **"config.php"** file via **"required_once("../../../config.php");"** necessary to identify the system's users via the functions, **"require_login()"** and **"isadminQ", "isteacher()", "iscreator()" or "isstudentQ".**

```php
<?php

    require_once('../config.php');
    require_once('../locallib.php');

    $sloodleerrors = array();

    print_header('Sloodle login zone', '', '', '', false, '', '', false, '');
    print_heading('Sloodle logon zone');

    $loginzoneurl = SLOODLE_WWWROOT.'/login/sl_loginzone.php';
    $pasteurl = $loginzoneurl.'?pwd='.sloodle_prim_password();

    require_login($course->id, false, $cm);
    if (isadmin()) {
        //print_simple_box('You need to tell your prim to use the following URL to talk
    } else {
        print_simple_box('You need admin privileges to access this page.', "center");
        //print_simple_box('You would normally need admin privileges to access this pag
        //print_simple_box('You need to tell your prim to use the following URL to talk
        exit;
    }
```

Figura 3.3.1 Example of the use of user identification functions (Porfiro, 2007)

The prototype has the following structure within the "blocks" folder.

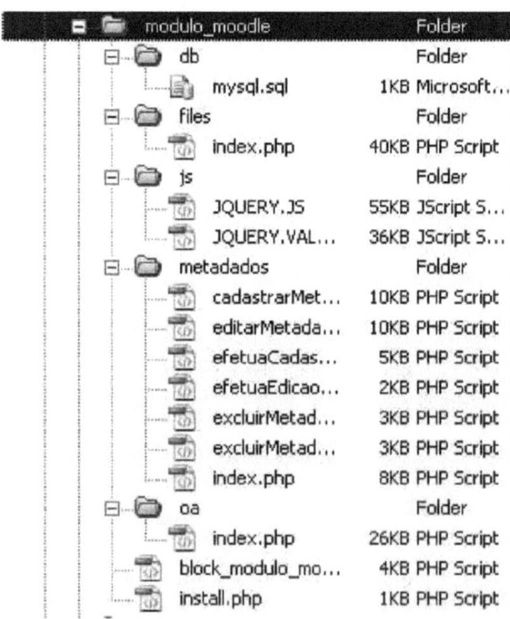

Figura 3.3.2 Basic structure of the prototype.

The "js" folder contains two JavaScript files, "jquery.js" and "jquery.validate.js". The jquery.js file contains a javascript library. This library has a huge number of defined functions and methods, which replace long and complex javascript codes with simple calls to the library's functions, making it easier to develop and reuse code, and enabling the use of a vast number of *plugins* created by other developers. The "jquery.validate.js" file is a *plugin for* "jquery.js", the purpose of which is to make it easier to validate forms. These two *JavaScript files* will be included in the ".php" files using the following line of code. Both files are available as free and open source software.

```
<script src="../js/JQUERY.JS" language="javascript">
        type="text/javascript"></script>

<script src="../js/JQUERY.VALIDATE.JS" language="javascript">
type="text/javascript"></script>
```

Figura 3.3.3 Adding the jQuery files.

The files folder has a file called "index.php". This file is exactly the same as the files folder at the root of Moodle, but it has an additional feature: it allows you to share material that is in the user's (teacher's) folder,

and has no metadata associated with it. This functionality is available in the table where the teacher's materials are listed, as shown in figure 3.3.4.

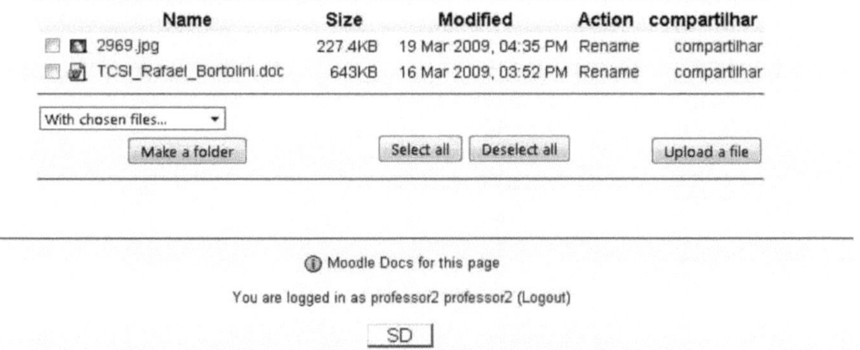

Figura 3.3.4 Modified index.php file from the files folder.

By clicking on share, the teacher is taken to the page for registering a new learning object and the material previously selected for sharing is copied and filled in automatically in the learning object field available on the form for registering new metadata. For this functionality to be available in the Moodle environment, the "index.php" file in the files folder, available in the modulo_moodle, must be copied and pasted into the files folder at the root of Moodle and replaced.

The "metadata" folder contains the files that will be used by the new module to register, change and delete metadata and learning objects. All the files in this folder use the "mdl_metadata" table. Each teacher has their own metadata, but the learning objects associated with this metadata automatically become public, with all the metadata registered by the teacher being listed in the "index.php" file. The "registerMetadata.php" file has a form where the teacher will register the new metadata and the learning object associated with it. When the teacher clicks on the "Send data" button, the data provided will be passed to the "registerMetadata.php", in this file the registration in the "mdl_metadata" table will actually take place, and the learning object will be sent to the "objectsLearning" folder, this folder is located outside the Moodle root, inside the "moodledata" folder. The "moodledata" folder is created automatically by the Moodle environment when it is installed, and the "learningobjects" folder is created automatically when the first learning object is registered.

There is only one file in the "oa" folder, which lists all the learning objects registered by all the teachers, including the teacher logged into the system. Using this file, the teacher can search for and add learning objects. The learning objects chosen by the teacher will be copied to the subject folder.

The tables created for this module must be added to the "mysql.sql" file and this file must be in the "db" folder, because we are using the Mysql database. If you want to use another database, add the "sql" scripts to a file with the name corresponding to the chosen database, for example, "postgresql.sql" if you are using PostgreSQL as your database. The figure below shows the code for the "mysql.sql" file. This file contains the following SQL commands, one for inserting a new record in the "mdl_block" table, another for creating a new table, and the others for creating relationships with the "mdl_user" and "mdl_block" tables.

```
INSERT INTO `mdl_block`
(`id`, `name`, `version`, `cron`, `lastcron`, `visible`, `multiple`)
VALUES
(NULL, 'modulo_moodle', '2007101509', '0', '0', '1', '0');


CREATE TABLE IF NOT EXISTS `mdl_metadados` (
  `idMetadados` int(11) NOT NULL AUTO_INCREMENT,
  `mdl_user_id` int(11) NOT NULL,
  `mdl_course_id` int(11) NOT NULL,
  `titulo` varchar(200) DEFAULT NULL,
  `sumario` varchar(200) DEFAULT NULL,
  `palavras_chave` varchar(200) DEFAULT NULL,
  `dificuldade` varchar(200) DEFAULT NULL,
  `linguagem` varchar(200) DEFAULT NULL,
  `objeto_aprendizagem` varchar(500) DEFAULT NULL,
  `extensao` varchar(10) DEFAULT NULL,
  `tamanho` varchar(200) DEFAULT '',
  PRIMARY KEY (`idMetadados`),
  UNIQUE KEY `idMetadados` (`idMetadados`)
) ENGINE=MyISAM  DEFAULT CHARSET=utf8 AUTO_INCREMENT=61 ;

ALTER TABLE `mdl_metadados` ENGINE = InnoDB;

ALTER TABLE `mdl_user` ENGINE = InnoDB;

ALTER TABLE `mdl_course` ENGINE = InnoDB;

ALTER TABLE `mdl_metadados` MODIFY COLUMN `mdl_user_id` BIGINT(10) UNSIGNED NOT NULL,
 MODIFY COLUMN `mdl_course_id` BIGINT(10) UNSIGNED NOT NULL
, ROW_FORMAT = DYNAMIC;

ALTER TABLE `mdl_metadados` ADD CONSTRAINT `FK_mdl_metadados_user` FOREIGN KEY `FK_mdl_metadados_user` (`mdl_user_id`)
    REFERENCES `mdl_user` (`id`)
    ON DELETE RESTRICT
    ON UPDATE RESTRICT
, ROW_FORMAT = DYNAMIC;

ALTER TABLE `mdl_metadados` ADD CONSTRAINT `FK_mdl_metadados_course` FOREIGN KEY `FK_mdl_metadados_course` (`mdl_course_id`)
    REFERENCES `mdl_course` (`id`)
    ON DELETE RESTRICT
    ON UPDATE RESTRICT
, ROW_FORMAT = DYNAMIC;

commit;
```

Figura 3.3.5 mysql.sql file

The file described above will only be used during the installation of the new module and will no longer be needed once the installation is complete. This file can have its code copied and executed directly in the MySQL database. To make installation easier, another file called "install.php" was created, which contains code for the automatic execution of the script called "mysql.sql". This script will create the mdl_metadata table and include the record in the mdl_block table, as well as the relationships with the "mdl_user" and "mdl_course" tables.

The figure below shows the "install.php" file

```php
<?php

    if(!file_exists("../../config.php")){
        header("Location ../../install.php");
        die;
    }

    require_once("../../config.php");

    if(file_exists($CFG->dirroot.'/course/lib.php')){
        require_once($CFG->dirroot.'/course/lib.php');
    }else
    {
        echo "lib.php nao existe";
    }

    if(!record_exists("block","name","modulo_moodle"))
    {
        $strdatabasesucess = get_string("databasesucess");

        if(file_exists($CFG->dirroot.'/blocks/modulo_moodle/db/'.$CFG->dbtype.'.sql')){
            $db->debug = true;

            modify_database("$CFG->dirroot/blocks/modulo_moodle/db/$CFG->dbtype.sql");

            $db->debug = false;

            notify($strdatabasesucess , "green");
        }else
        {
            echo "arquivo db nao existe";
        }
    }

    redirect("/moodle/" , $strdatabasesucess , 1);

?>
```

Figura 3.3.6 Install.php file

Now let's run the "install.php" file to install the new module. To do this, the files described in "figure 4.1" above must all be inside a folder, in this example the name of the folder is "modulo_moodle" and this folder is inside the "blocks" folder. Installation consists of creating the tables that will be used by the prototype, and inserting a new record into the "mdl_block" table, which contains the records of all the *blocks* registered in the system. If the record is not present in the "mdl_block" table, the new module will not be listed and cannot be included.

To start the installation, access the 'install.php" file via the following uri: http://localhost/moodle/blocks/modulo moodle/install.php.

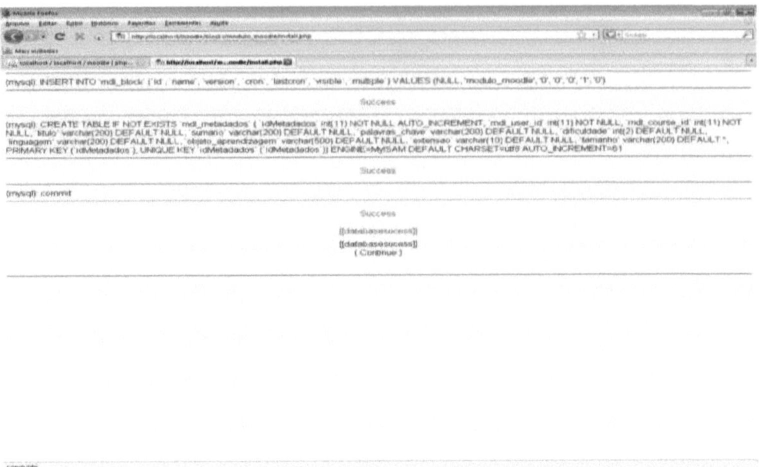

Figura 3.3.7 Prototype installation screen (install.php).

Once the installation is complete, we can see that the "mdl_block" table has a new record, as shown in the figure below.

			id	name	version	cron	lastcron	visible	multiple
			31	tags	2007101509	0	0	1	1
			37	modulo_moodle	2007101509	0	0	1	0

Figura 3.3.8 mdl_block" table after installation.

To complete the installation we need to access the "Notifications" page available in the administrator's main menu.

Figura 3.3.9 Notification page - only available to the administrator.

Now we can include the new module, by logging in as a teacher or administrator, accessing the course to be used and clicking *on "Turn editing on"* in the "Administration" menu. This button enables the editing and inclusion of other *blocks, so* now we can include the new *block* as shown below.

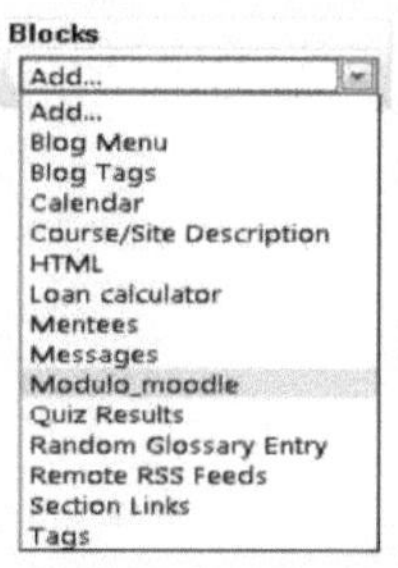

Figura 3.3.10 adding a new block

Once the new module has been added, the block will be available on the course's home page. The file responsible for displaying the links is "block_modulo_moodle.php".

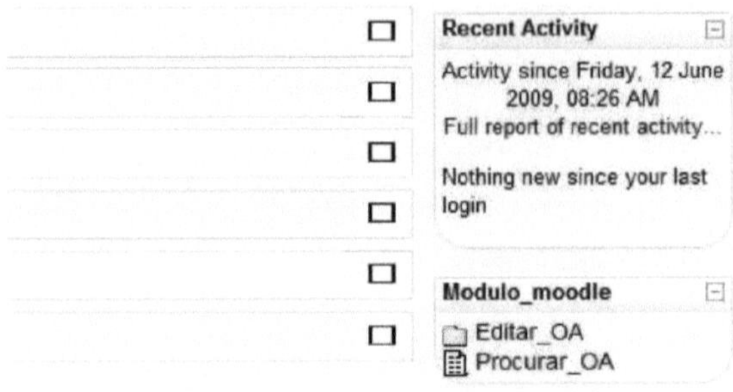

Figura 3.3.11 Course home screen.

Figure 3.3.12 shows the tool's implementation diagram.

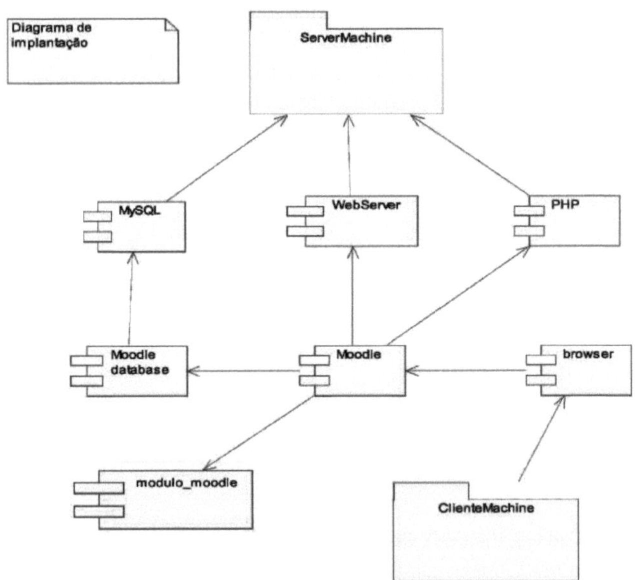

Figure 3.3.12 Deployment diagram.

3.4 Example of prototype use

This topic will show an example of the use of the prototype created, so that the work can be presented in operation.

The following scenario was created as an example. Two classes with the names "Distributed Systems" and "Database B" and two teachers with the names "teacher2" and "teacher" respectively associated with these classes. The idea is to register a metadata and associate it with a learning object.

What will be used in practice will be the learning object, but in order to find this object among so many others we have to use the metadata associated with this object.

Figura 3.4.1 -Moodle home screen

In this first example, we will log in to the system with the user "teacher". After *logging in,* we click on "metadata" available in the "administration" menu. The screen below is then displayed.

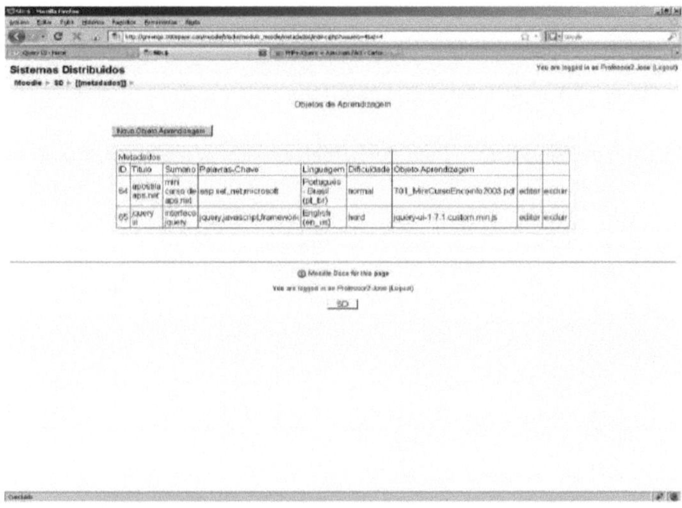

Figura 3.4.2 - Table of learning objects

Now click on the button located just above the table called "new metadata". The form shown in the figure below is then displayed.

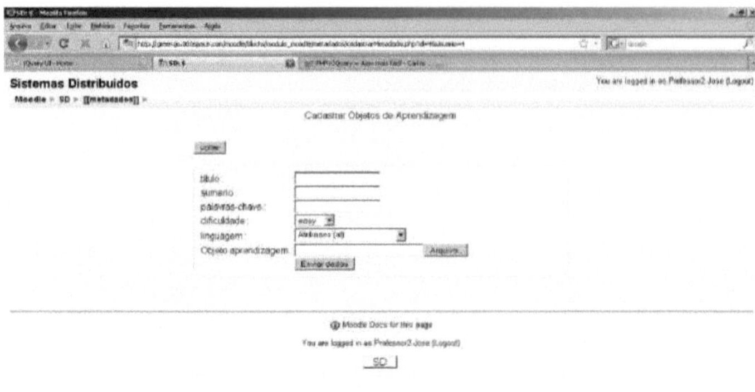

Figura 3.4.3 - Metadata registration form.

Fill in all the fields and click on the "send data" button. A new metadata is now registered, as you can see in the screen below:

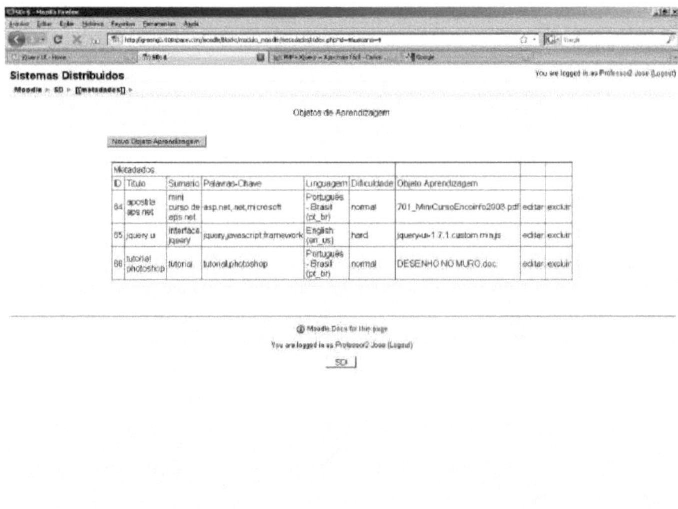

Figura 3.4.4 - oa table after inserting new metadata.

Now let's *log in* again with the other user, "teacher2", and click on "LearningObjects". On this screen we see that the metadata registered by the "teacher" user is available. In order to use this learning object, we first have to select the item by clicking on the "checkBox" on the left-hand side of the object, then select the "includeFile" option from the drop-down list below the file table. In this example we only have one learning object, but if the quantity is too large we have the option of searching for the learning object using a text box located just above the table, in this box we can locate the object by typing in a keyword or part of it, as well as typing in the name or part of it, there is also another filter option which is the file extension, it is not necessary for the teacher to enter this information as it is filled in automatically.

Figura 3.4.5 - List of all learning objects.

After selecting the "includeFile" option, the screen below will appear.

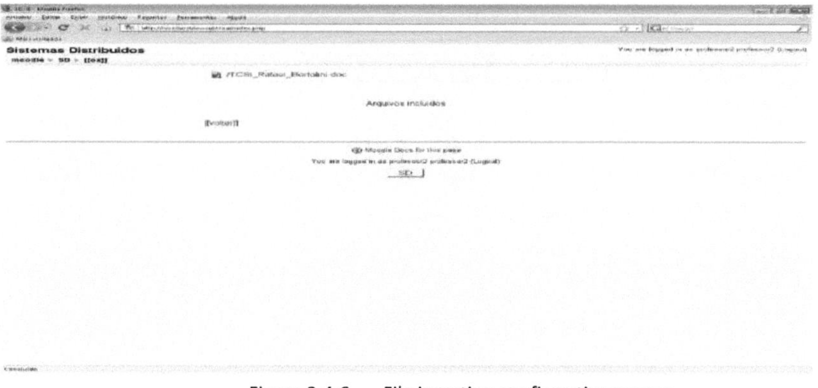

Figura 3.4.6 - File insertion confirmation screen.

We can now use the learning object at any time in this course. We can check this by clicking on "Files" available in the "Administration" menu.

Figura 3.4.7 - Table of files.

Another feature is to share a learning object that has already been registered but has no metadata associated with it. To share it, simply click on "Files" in the "Administration" menu.

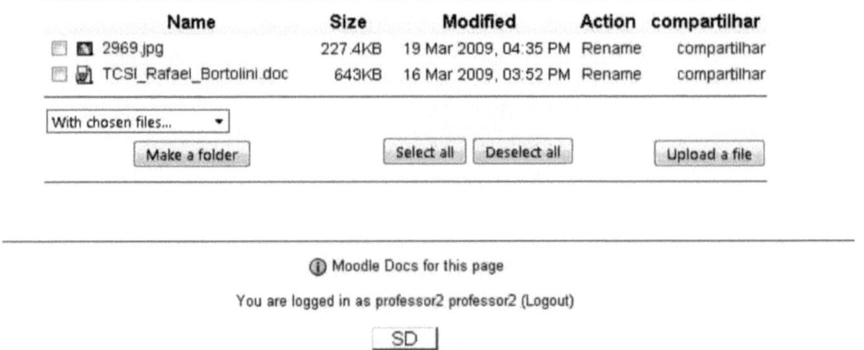

Figura 3.4.8 - Table of files.

This screen shows all the files available to the subject teacher. To share, simply click on "share" in the file table in the last column on the right.

After clicking on "share", the user is shown the screen below so that a new metadata can be associated with the previously selected learning object. The "Learning object" field is automatically filled in with the file selected from the file table. Simply fill in the data and click on "Send data".

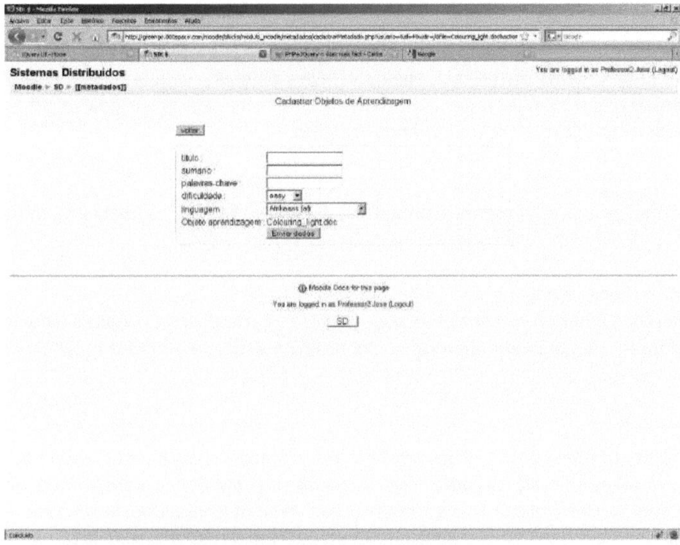

Figure 3.4.9 - Form for registering new metadata.

3.5 Usability evaluation using ErgoList

Section 3.5 aims to verify the interface created for the prototype and test it using ErgoList.

The ErgoList project aims to conceive, design, develop and make available via the Web/Internet a tool for the autonomous evaluation of the user-friendliness of interactive software devices (Ergolist, 2009).

The checklists used here make up a rapid assessment technique. They are intended to support the inspection of the interface and uncover its most glaring ergonomic defects. More detailed evaluations involving complex interfaces should be carried out by ergonomists using heuristic techniques and/or user interaction tests (Ergolist, 2009).

The following checklists were used to evaluate the prototype:

- **Protection against errors**
  Error protection refers to the mechanisms used to detect and prevent errors in data entries, commands, possible actions with disastrous and/or non-recoverable consequences.

- **User experience**
  Consideration of the user experience concerns the means implemented that allow the system to respect the user's level of experience.

- **Error messages**
  The quality of the messages refers to the relevance, legibility and accuracy of the information given to the user, the nature of the error made (syntax, format, etc.) and the actions to be taken to correct it.

- **Compatibility**
  The compatibility criterion refers to the agreement that may exist between the user's characteristics (memory, perception, habits, skills, age, expectations, etc.) and the tasks, on the one hand, and the organisation of the outputs, inputs and dialogue of a given application, on the other. It also concerns the degree of similarity between different environments and applications.

- **Flexibility**
  Flexibility refers to the means made available to the user that allow them to personalise the interface to take account of the requirements of the task, their strategies or their working habits. It also corresponds to the number of different ways available to the user to achieve a certain goal. In other words, the interface's ability to adapt to the user's various actions.

- **Error correction**
  The error correction criterion concerns the means made available to the user to enable them to correct their errors.

- **Homogeneity/Coherence (Consistency)**
  The homogeneity/coherence criterion refers to the way in which interface design choices (codes, names, formats, procedures, etc.) are kept identical in identical contexts and different in different contexts.

- **Immediate feedback**
  Immediate Feedback refers to the system's responses to the user's actions. Such inputs can range from the simple press of a key to a list of commands. In all cases, computer responses must be provided quickly, with appropriate and consistent timing for each type of transaction. In any case, a quick response must be provided with information about the requested transaction and its result.

3.5.1 Evaluation results using ErgoList

After using Ergolist to check the prototype's conformity, we put together the table below to present the final report.

Table 3.5.1: Evaluation results using Ergolist

Criteria	Total Questions	Answered	Not answered	Compliant Issues	Non-conforming questions	Not Applicable Questions	Quest. Postponed	%
Error protection	7	7	0	1	3	3	0	25%
User Experience	6	6	0	2	1	3	0	75%
Error messages	9	9	0	5	4	0	0	55%
Compatibility	21	21	0	6	0	15	0	100%
Flexibility	3	3	0	1	2	0	0	25%
Error correction	5	5	0	1	0	4	0	100%
Consistency	11	11	0	10	0	1	0	100%
Feedback	12	12	0	7	5	0	0	59%
Total	74	74	0	33	15	26	0	68%

To finalise the evaluation, we'll only consider the questions that apply to the prototype, disregarding the column of questions that don't apply to the prototype, and then fill in the last column (which represents the prototype's compliance percentage).

After carrying out the calculations, we can conclude that the usability of the prototype is 68 per cent in line with ErgoList. Using the table, we can conclude that the weak points and candidates for improvement are: error protection and flexibility, respectively.

CHAPTER 4

FINAL CONSIDERATIONS

The aim of this final paper is to show how the use of learning objects in distance learning provides quality continuing education, which significantly enhances learning. Just as important as the use and suitability of these objects for teaching and learning are the choice of environment to be used and the form of support given to students.

The initiative to create a repository of learning objects for reuse is not an isolated one, but is in line with international trends.

The reuse of learning objects, as well as their adaptation and modification by teachers, means that the same material can be used in various contexts and can be adapted to the interests, needs and specificities of each new group of students.

I hope that this work will mainly benefit the area of Distance Education, which is currently being used by large universities such as PUCRS. But although the study of this environment is aimed at sharing learning objects, I would like this study to collaborate mainly with the process of developing new functionalities for the Moodle environment, as well as with developers who want more information about the development process for the environment. Systematising and organising information in such a way as to speed up the study of those interested in developing new functionalities.

"It's true that the school is an institution that for five thousand years has been based on the teacher's talking/dictating, the pupil's handwriting and, for four centuries, a moderate use of printing. A true integration of information technology means abandoning an anthropological habit that is more than a thousand years old, which cannot be done in a few years." Levi (1993)

Future work

It is believed that many others on this subject will follow this model and complement it with new comments and tips to help the Moodle community, especially the Brazilian community, to make this tool better and more complete.

Functionalities can be added or complemented, and one possibility for future work would be to develop a new prototype that allows learning objects to be shared with different Moodle environments, not restricted to an isolated system. The idea is to place a repository of learning objects outside all Moodle environments, a universal repository that would allow access from all environments.

CHAPTER 5

REFERENCES

Morais, Alana, 2008. Metadata for learning objects. Available at: <http://www.intv.cefetce.br/connepi/papers/db604fc7d5b8730fbf04a0651ca8.pdf>. Accessed on: 17 March 2009

(ADL) Advanced Distributed Learning, 2003 . Available at: http://www.adlnet.org. Accessed on 18 June 2009

Bertoletti-De-Marchi, Ana Carolina, 2004. A proposal for a metadata standard for science and technology museum learning objects. Available at: <http://www.cinted.ufrgs.br/renote/mar2004/artigos/02-umapropostadepadrao.pdf>.
Accessed on 15 Mar. 2009

AICC, 2008. Aviation industry cbt committee. Available at: <http://www.aicc.org> Accessed on: 02 Sep. 2008

AulaNet, 2007. AulaNet. Father Leonel Franca Foundation - PUC-Rio. Available at: <http://www.aulanet.com.br>

Raymond, Eric S, 1999 . The Digital Revolution and the Knowledge Society. Available at: <http://www.ime.usp.br/~is/ddt/mac333/aulas/tema-6-15abr99.html>. Accessed on: 03 June 2008

Bohl, O., J. Scheuhase, et al, 2002. The sharable content object reference model (SCORM). A critical review. International Conference on Computers in Education (ICCE02), Auckland, New Zealand. IEEE Press, 2002.

Benedito, Miguel, 2005 XML - *Extensible Markup Language.* Available at: <http://www.gta.ufrj.br/grad/OO_I/miguel/>. Accessed on: 20 March 2008.

CNED, 2009 . Author. Available at: <http://www.cenedcursos.com.br/atutor/about.php>. Accessed on: 20 September 2008

CHIN, 2002. Canadian Heritage Information NetWork. Available at: <http://www.chin.gc.ca/>. Accessed on 03 June 2008.

Downes, Stephen, 2001 *"Learning Objects: Resources for Distance Education Worldwide".* IN: International Review of Research in Open and Distance Learning. Available at: <http://www.irrodl.Org/content/v2.l/downes.pdf>. Accessed on: 22 October 2008.

EUREKA, 2007. A web-based co-operative learning environment for distance learning. Available at: <http://eureka.pucpr.br/>. Accessed on 07 October 2008.

FirstClass, 2007. *Powering collaborative online communities.* Available at: <http://softarc.com>. Accessed on: 03 September 2008.

IEEE, 2002. Draft Standard for Learning Object Metadata. Available at: <http://ltsc.ieee.org/wgl2/files/LOM_1484_12_I_vl_Final_Draft.pdf>. Accessed on: 18 Nov. 2008.

IMS, 2005. IMS *Learning Design,* evolving from Learning Objects to Learning Activities. Available at: <http://www.lume.ufrgs.br/bitstream/handle/10183/13008/000573000.pdf>. Accessed on: 19 September

2008.

Ergolist. 2009, Ergolist Project. Available at: <http://www.labiutil.inf.ufsc.br/ergolist/projeto.htm>. Accessed on 05 June 2008.

Jaime Balbino, 2007 Objetos de Aprendizagem: Contribuições para sua genealogia. Available at: <http://www.dicas-.com.br/educacao_tecnologia/print/educacao_tecnologia_20070423.html> Accessed on 07 May 2008.

LOPES, Laura M C, CASANOVA, Marco A, 2004. Development of web-based courses: a methodological proposal.

Machado, Glaucio José Couri,2003. Virtual learning environments: dialogue and processes of subjectivation. Available at:<http://www.anped.org.br/reunioes/27/gtl6/tl64.pdf>. Accessed on: 19 March 2008.

Moodle. 2009. Available at: <http://www.moodle.org>.

MUZIO, 2001. J.; HEINS, T.; MUNDELL, R. *Experiences with Reusable eLearning Objects: From Theory to Practice.* Victoria, Canada.

Rosa, Núbia Santos, 2008. A Proposed Model for Learning Objects Available at: <http://www.prodepa.gov.br/sbc2008/anais/pdf/arq0028.pdf>. Accessed on: 12 Nov. 2008.

Olsen, G. S, 2002. *Standy Ready? Emerging e-learning standards in a pedagogical perspective.* Available at: <http://www.nettskolen.com/forskning/standards.pdf>. Accessed on: 22 September 2008.

Otsuka, Joice Lee. Support for Formative Assessment in the TelEduc Distance Education Environment, 2002. Available at:<http://www.dcc.unicamp.br/~rlachi/artigos/18_jrth_ie2002.pdf>. Accessed on: 18 September 2008.

PORTO, F. MOURA, A.M.C.; FERNANDEZ, 2003. A data model and query language for e- learning objects, Proc. Rio de Janeiro: PGL Research Conference.

Porfiro, Roberto Martins, 2007. A tool for managing groups by student profile in the Moodle environment.

SCORM, 2008 . Formative assessment through SCORM/AICC activities. Available at: <http://penta3.ufrgs.br/SCORM/tutorialAvalFormMoodleSCORM.html>. Accessed on: 23 May 2008.

Sosteric, Nike & Hesemeier, Susan, 2008. "When is a Learning Object not an Object: a first step towards a theory of learning objects". IN: International Review of Research in Open and Distance Learning.

Souza, Antonio Carlos dos Santos, 2005. Collaborative Learning Objects Available at: <http://www.abed.org.br/congresso2005/por/pdf/024tcc4.pdf>. Accessed on: 08 March 2008.

TAROUCO, Liane Margarida, Grando, Anita Raquel, Fabre, Marie-Christine, Konrath, Mary Pedroso, 2004, L.M.R. Objetos de Aprendizagem para M-Learning. Available at: <http://www.cinted.ufrgs.br/CESTA/objetosdeaprendizagem sucesu.pdf>. Accessed on: 14 September 2008.

W3C, 2003. World wide web consortium. Available at: <http://www.w3.org>.

WebCT, 2000 .Web Course Tools. Available at:

<http://www.dca.fee.unicamp.br/proiects/sapiens/Reports/rf2000/node23.html>. Accessed on: 21 Nov. 2008.

WILEY, D.A, 2001. The Instructional Use of Learning Objects. Wiley & Sons.(Ed). Available at: <http://reusabilitv.org/read/chapter/wiley.doc>. Accessed on 28 October 2008.

CHAPTER 6

Appendix A - Tools used to implement the prototype.

The purpose of the following document is to explain which tools are used during the implementation phase and how to install and use them.

B.I Moodle installation resources

Before installing the Moodle environment, you'll need to install a server that supports PHP, as Moodle is entirely developed using this language, and you'll also need a database manager, usually using MySQL.

We suggest using the XAMPP installer, which has all these requirements in a single installation. This installer can be downloaded from http://www.apachefriends.org/en/xampp.html. Obtain the installer and carry out the installation in accordance with its installation manual, which can be found on the same page as the installer download - http://www.apachefriends.org/pt br/xampp-windows.htmL Once this installation has been carried out, access it via the web browser - http://localhost/, the main XAMPP screen should appear as shown in Figure B.I.

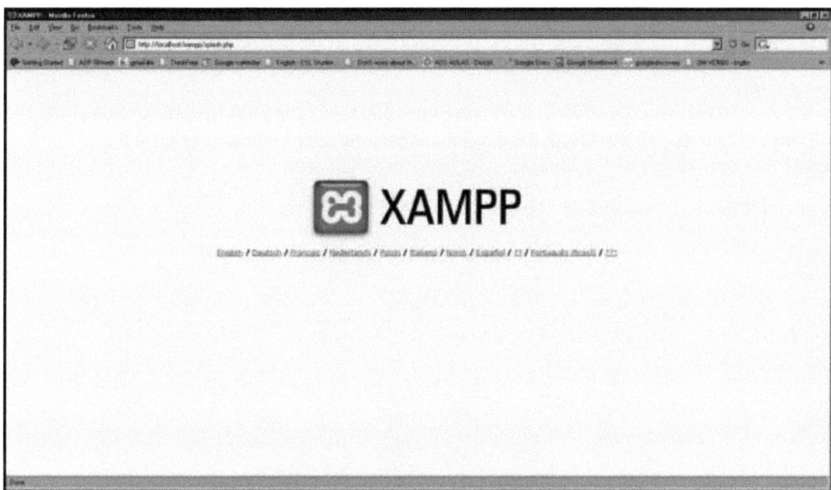

Figure B.I-The XAMPP start screen.

On this screen we can choose the language that will be used in XAMPP, after choosing the language the screen below will appear.

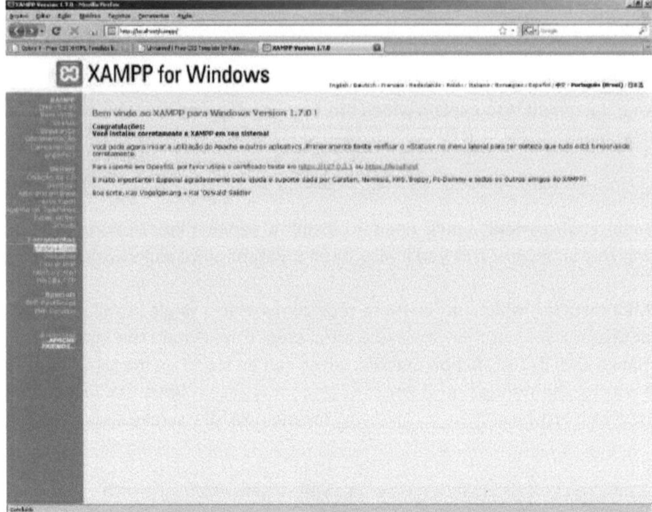

Figura 8.2 - XAMPP main menu.

From the XAMPP main menu, which is shown in Figure B.2, select the phpMyAdmin option under the "Tools" menu, this will take you to the Mysql database management screen, shown in Figure B.3.

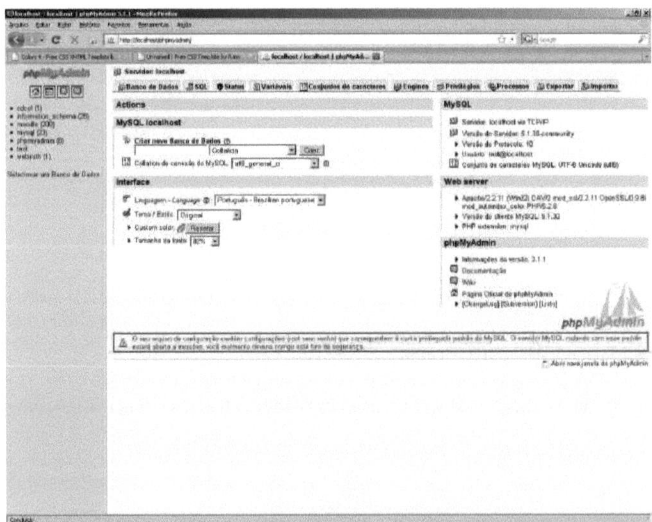

Figura 8.3 - phpMyAdmin home screen

(MySQL database manager).

The database manager comes by default with a registered user, the "root" user. This user has no password associated with him, so it is highly recommended that you set a password for this user. To do this, click on the variables tab in the phpMyAdmin start menu.

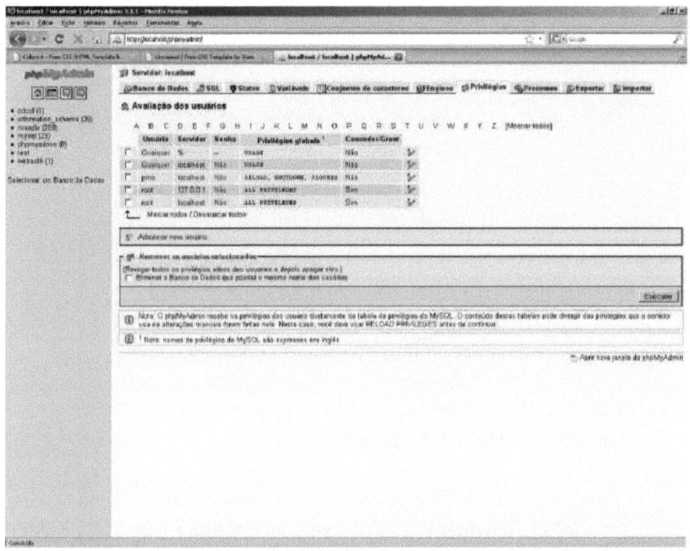

Figura 8.4 MySQL user management screen.

On this screen you can set the password for the root user, and you can also create a new user for the database.

After setting the password for the "root" user or creating a new user, let's now create a new database that will host the Moodle tables.

There are two ways to create a new database, one available from the phpMyAdmin home screen where you simply type in the name of the new database and click on the "Create" button, and the other available from the "SQL" tab, where you can include SQL code directly in the database.

Actions
MySQL localhost
Criar novo Banco de Dados
moodle Collation Criar
Collation de conexão do MySQL: utf8_general_ci
Interface
Linguagem - *Language*: Português - Brazilian portuguese
Tema / Estilo: Original
Custom color: Resetar
Tamanho da fonte: 82%

Figure B.5 - New database creation screen.

After clicking on create the following screen will appear.

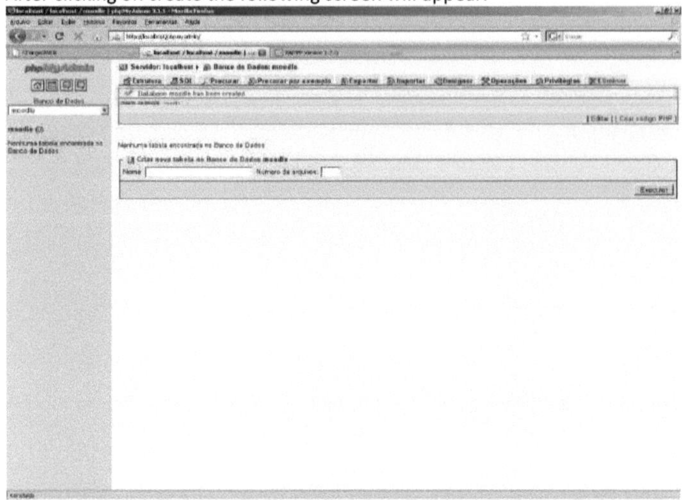

Figura 8.6 - New database created.

That's it. Now we have a complete environment for Moodle. To get started, download the Moodle packages available at www.moodle.org. After "downloading" the environment, unzip it into the XAMPP "htdocs" folder - this is where the ".php" files should be.

You can then start the Moodle installation. To do this, go to the following address in your browser http://localhost/moodle/install.php and the screen B.7 will be displayed.

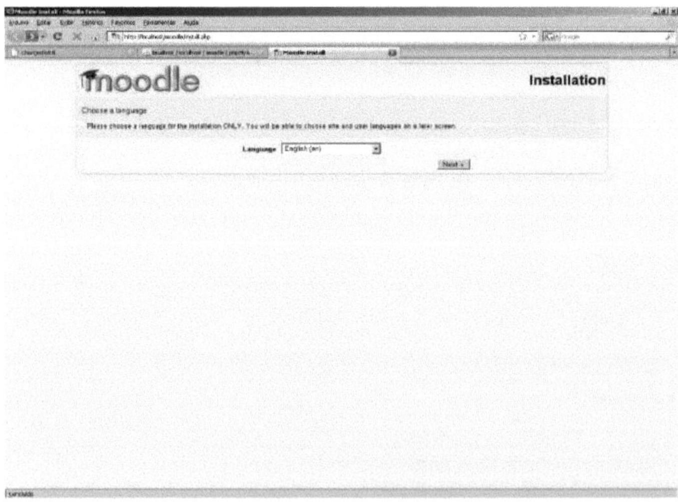

Figura 8.7 - Initial Moodle installation screen.

Select the language you want to use from the combo box and click "next" to proceed with the installation.

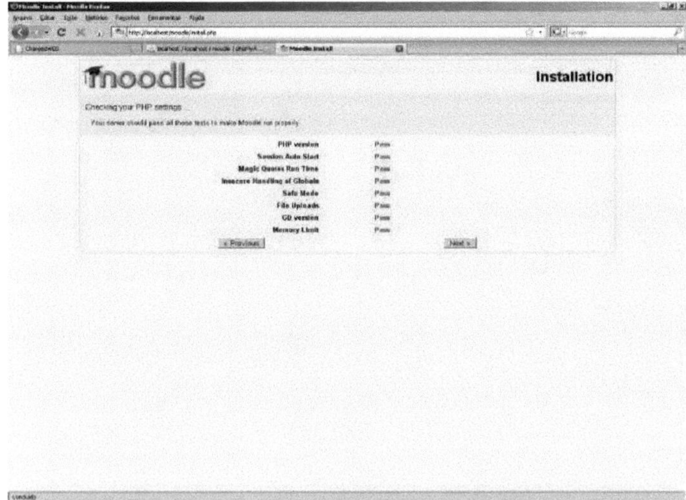

Figura 8.8 - System check screen.

In this part of the installation, the installer will check that the system that will receive Moodle has the PHP module installed and configured correctly. If everything is "OK" click on "next", on the next screen set the web address and the data directory.

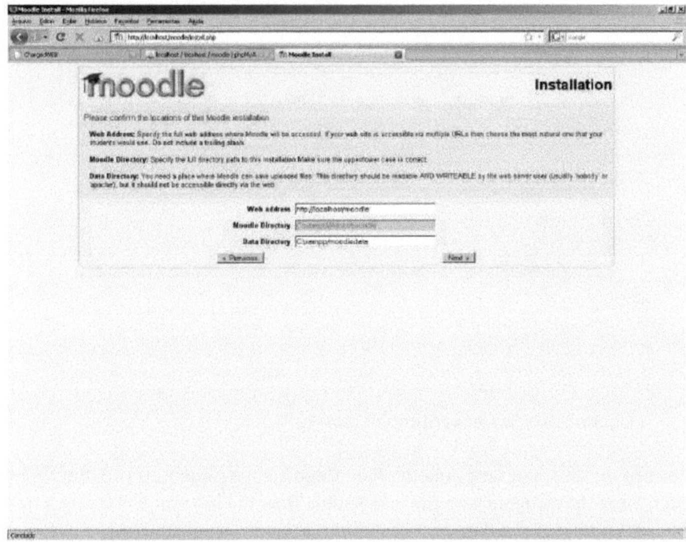

Figura 8.9 - Directories definition screen.

On the next screen, define the information relating to the MySQL database, such as the user, password, database name and prefix of the tables that will be created. Configure everything and click "next"

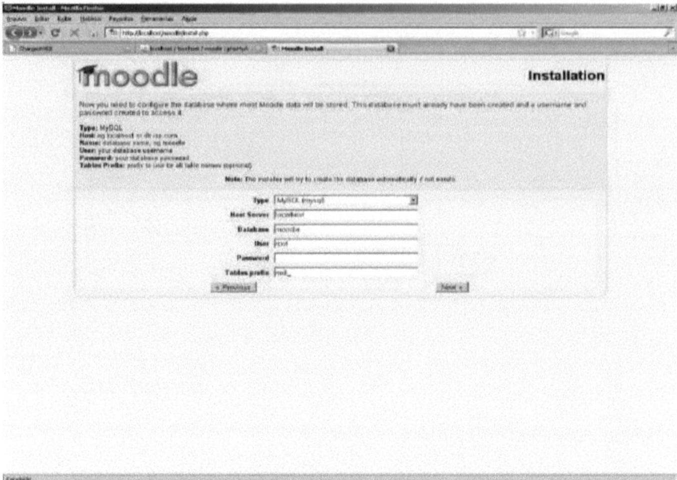

Figura 8.10 MySQL data definition screen.

A new test will be carried out to check the various components of the server.

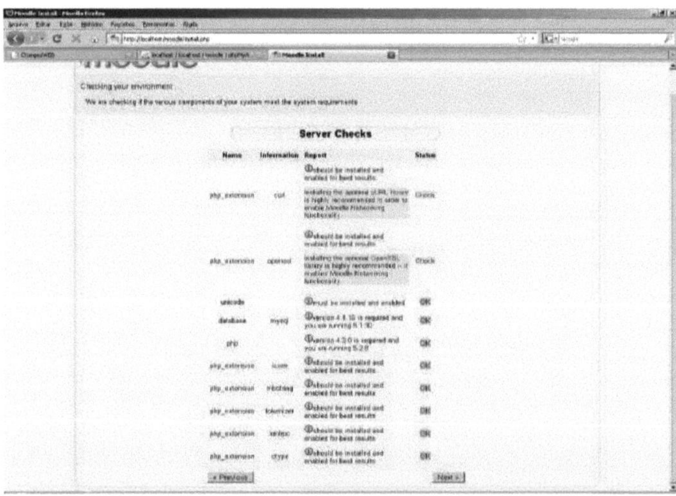

Figure B.10 - Server verification screen.

On the next screen you can install a new language for your Moodle environment. If you don't want to install another language, click "next" to continue with the installation. Now the installer will create a new file called "config.php", this file will contain all the data provided during the installation and will be available at the root of Moodle.

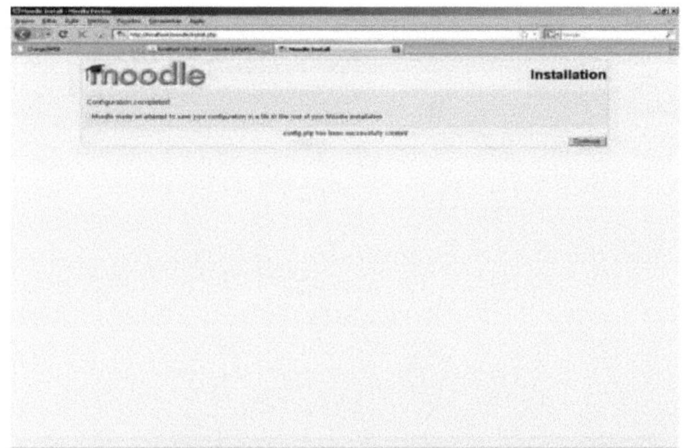

Figura 8.10 Confirmation screen for the creation of the config.php file.

After creating the "config.php" file, the installer will show the screen below, on which it will display the licence terms for the Moodle environment.

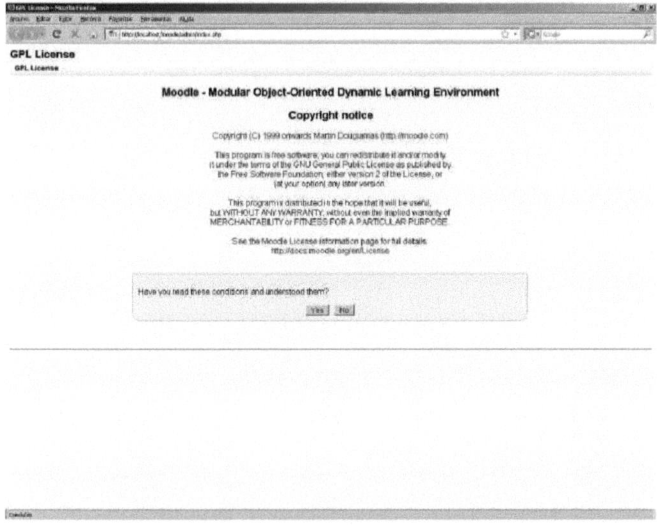

Figura 8.11 - Moodle licence screen.

Once the licence has been accepted, a new screen will be displayed showing information about the version of the environment that will be installed, as shown in figure B.12.

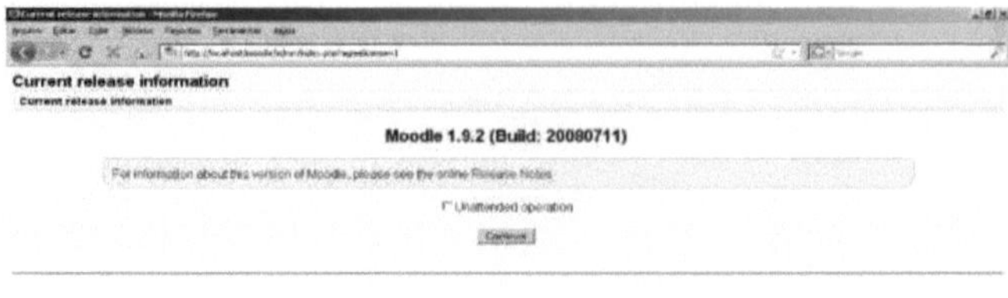

Figura 8.12 - Screen for the version of the system to be installed.

Click on "continue" to start the installation. In the next few screens, the tables will be created; there are 198 tables in all.

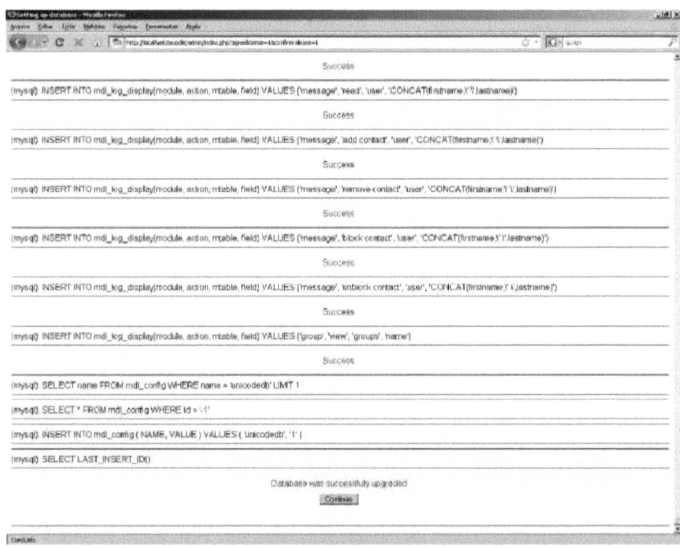

Figura 8.13 - Table creation screen.

Click on "continue" to go to the next screen.

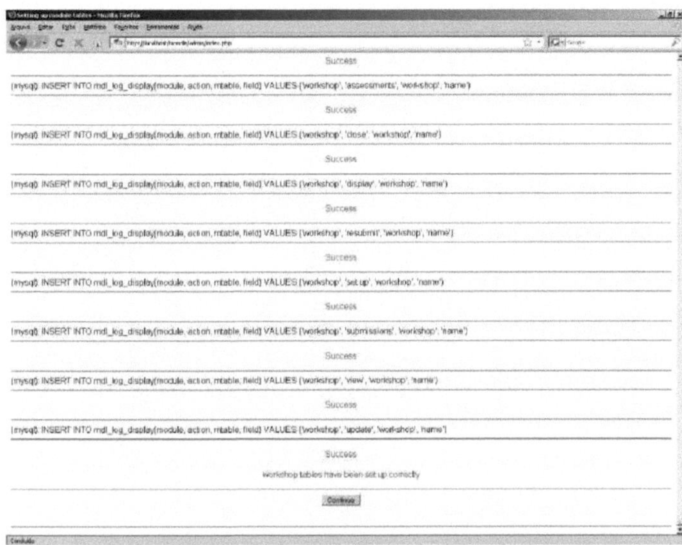

Figura 8.14 - Table creation screen.

Click on "continue" to go to the next screen.

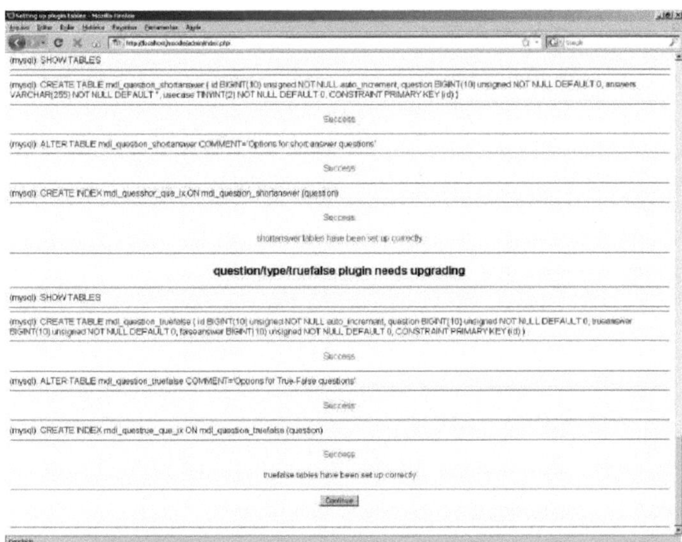

Figure B.15 - Module table creation screen.

Click on "continue" to go to the next screen.

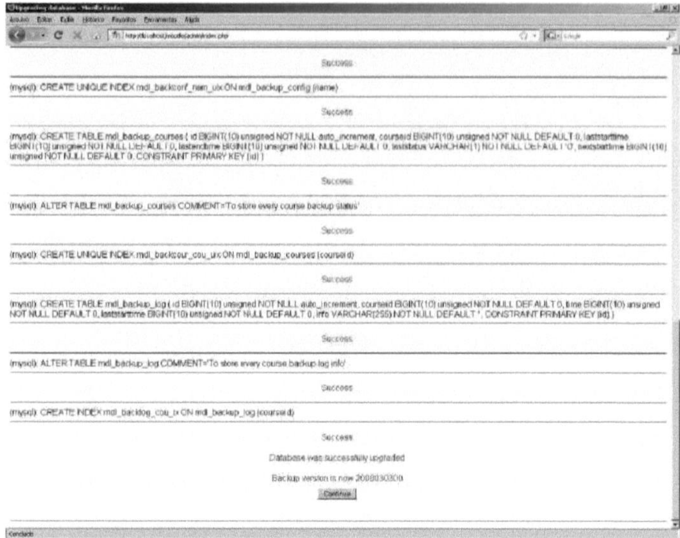

Figure B.16-Table creation screen

Figure B.17 - Configuring the environment's box tables

From now on, we'll configure the system administrator's details, such as password, e-mail address and username.

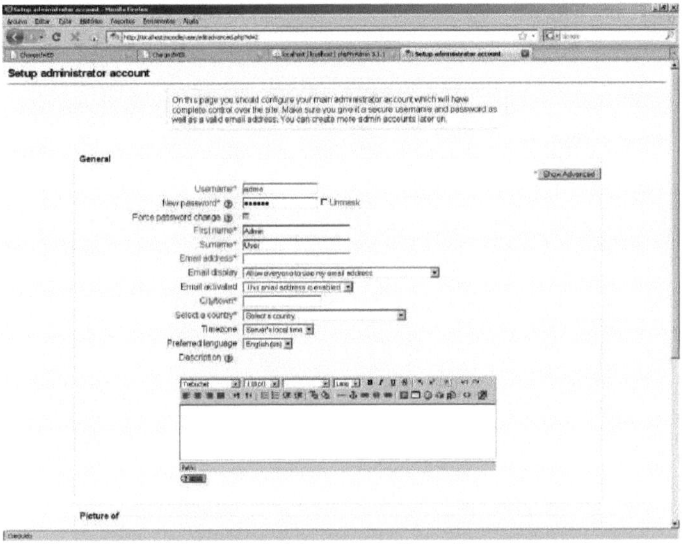

Figura 8.18 System administrator configuration screen

On this screen we will configure the data for the Moodle home page, such as the name that will be used in the environment, fill in the data and click on "save changes". The installation of the Moodle environment is now complete, as shown in figure B.20.

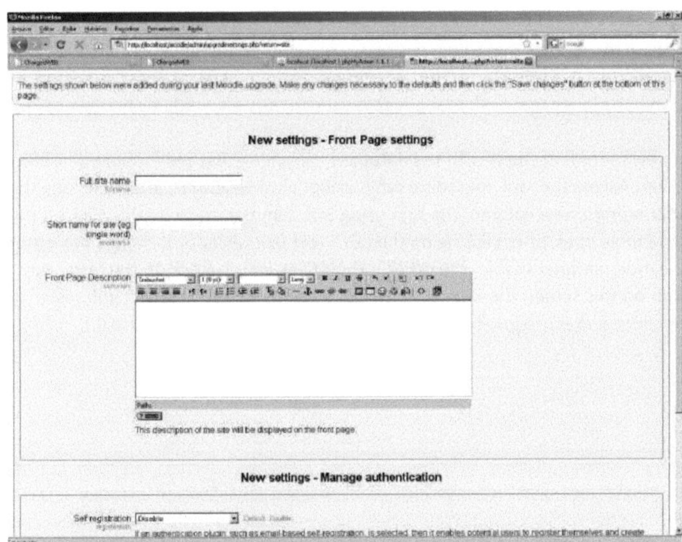

Figura 8.19 - System front configuration screen.

Figura 8.20 Main screen of the installed Moodle environment.

Appendix B - Modifying and creating metadata.

The following document explains how to add new metadata to the new module and how to change existing metadata.

C.I Adding new metadata.

Before I start explaining how to add new metadata, it is highly recommended that you fulfil two basic requirements, firstly to read appendix A available in this document and to have at least a notion of programming, preferably using the php language, as this language is used in the new module and throughout the Moodle environment.

The first step in adding new metadata starts with the database, assuming that the module is already installed and running on the server. Access the mdl_metadata table using "phpMyAdmin", after selecting the table there are two options for creating a new column, the first using SQL commands, to do this click on the "SQL" tab available just above the table data, after clicking on the tab a text box will appear, in this box enter the SQL command to modify the mdl_metadata table, the other, simpler option is to click on the "structure" tab available next to the SQL tab on this screen the new column can be added visually, making it easier to create the new table, to do this click on execute just below the column listing as shown in figure C.I.

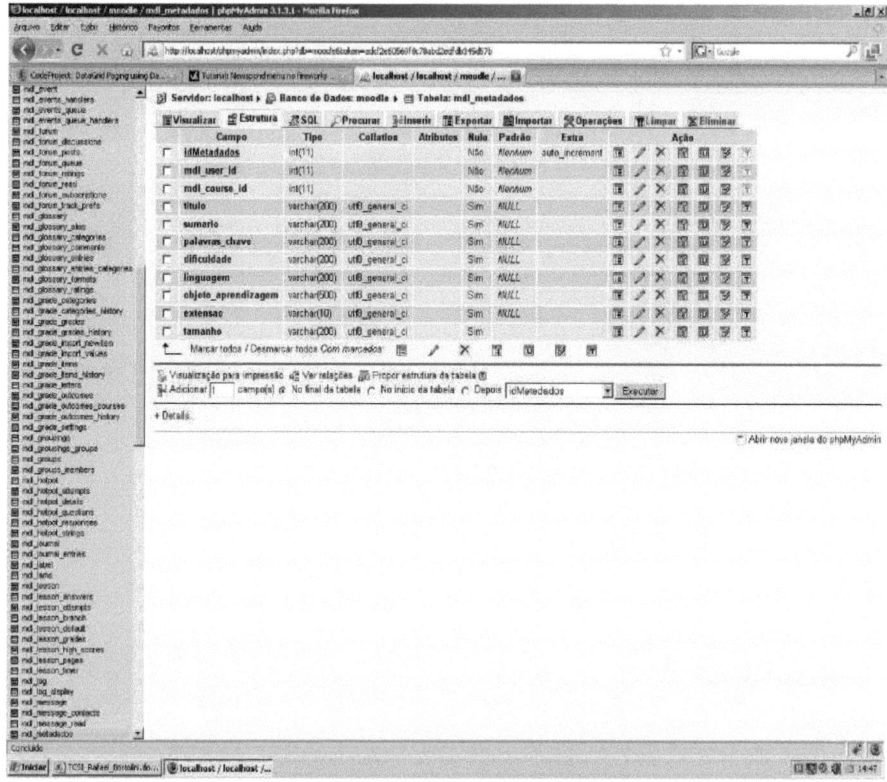

Figure C.l - Structure screen of the mdl_metadata table.

After clicking on execute a new screen will be shown, on this screen provide the data for creating the new column, as shown in figure C.2. For this example we will call the new column "new_field". After filling in the data click on "save". The table is ready.

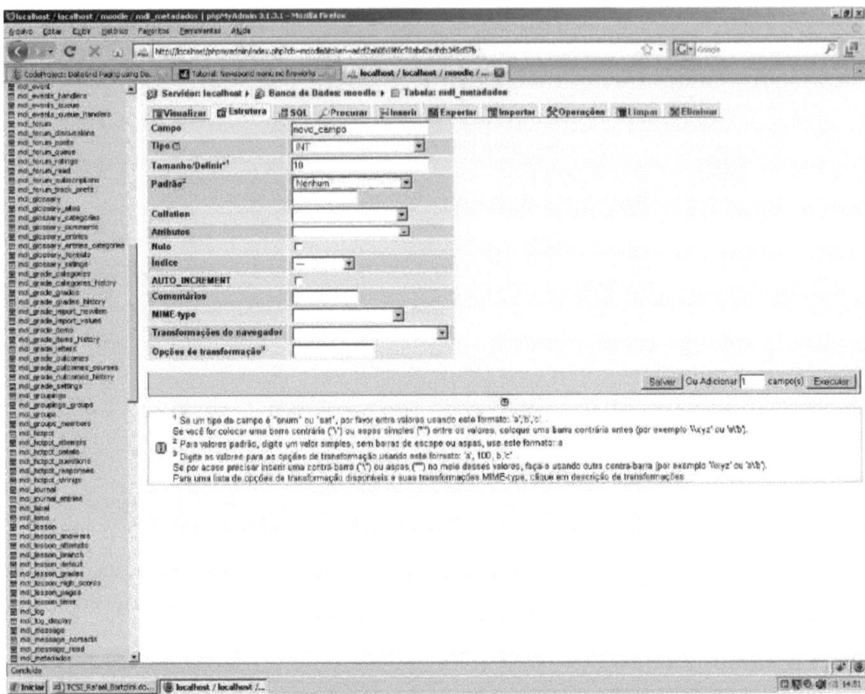

Figura 8.15 2 - Adding a new column to the mdl_metadata table.

Now let's edit the php files, the first file to edit is "cadastrarMetadado.php" from the metadata folder, in this file edit the available form and add the code below to create a new field.

```
//codigo para o novo campo.
echo "<tr>";
echo "<td>Novo campo :</td>";
echo "<td><input type=\"text\" name=\"novo_campo\"></td>";
echo "</tr>";
```

After inserting the code above, edit the file "efetuaCadastroMetadado.php" also in the metadata folder. This file will be responsible for actually inserting the data into the mdl_metadata table. In this file you will need to retrieve the form data from the file "cadastrarMetadado.php", to do this add the following command:

```
$novo_campo = $_POST['novo_campo'];.
```

This command will be responsible for retrieving the data entered into the form. All you have to do is edit the variable called "$query". There are two occurrences, the first used when the learning object field was filled in using the file upload and the other occurrence when the field was filled in using the share learning object option, available in the index.php file in the files folder, so it will be necessary to modify both occurrences of the '$query" variable. Figure C.3 shows the form with the new field.

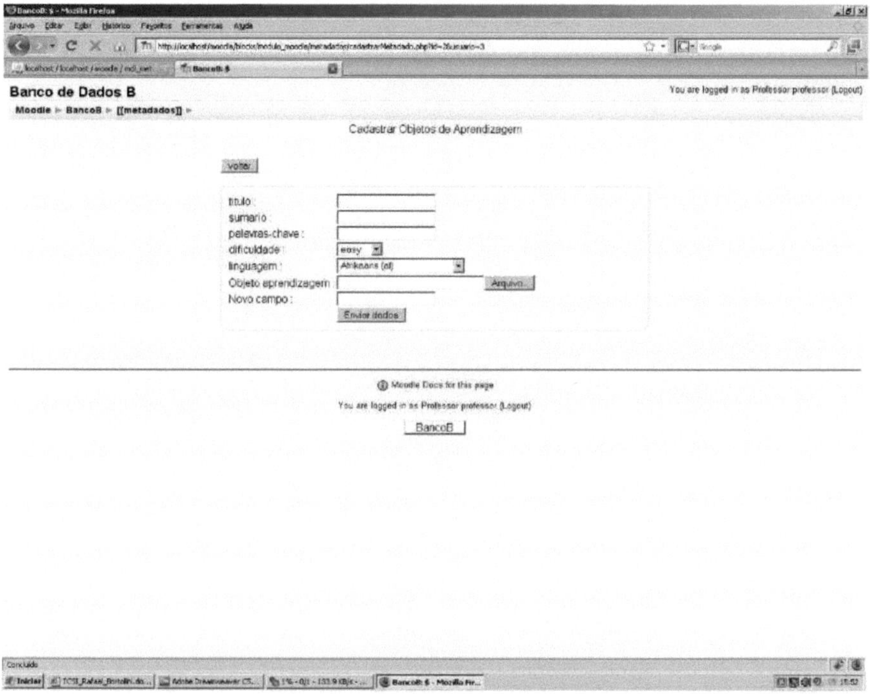

Figure C.3 - Modified registration form.

After completing the creation of the new field, we recommend changing the two php files responsible for editing the data, as the changed php files are only responsible for registering new metadata. Let's start by editing the "editMetadata.php" file in the metadata folder. The first change is to add a new field to the form available in the file. Add the code snippet below:

```
//codigo para editar novo campo.
echo "<tr>";
echo "<td>Novo campo :</td>";
echo "<td><input type=\"text\" name=\"novo_campo\"
value=".$row['novo_campo']."></td>";
echo "</tr>";
```

After adding the above code snippet, let's now change the "efetuaEdicaoMetadado.php" file, also in the metadata folder. In this file, add the following code snippet: `$novo_campo = $_POST['novo_campo'];`. ;. The purpose of this snippet is to retrieve the data entered in the previously created field. Now just change the "`$query`" variable. In the code snippet below, you can see the "`$query`" variable.

```
$query = "update mdl_metadados set titulo = '$titulo', dificuldade = '$dificuldade' ,
linguagem = '$linguagem', sumario = '$sumario', palavras_chave = '$palavraChave' ,
novo_campo = '$novo_campo' where idMetadados = $idMetadado";
```

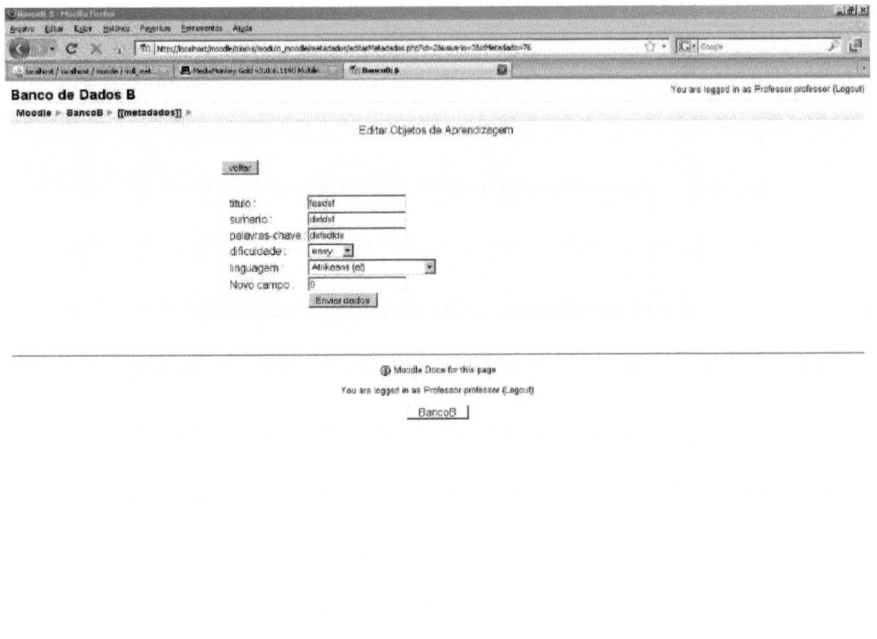

Figure C.4 - Modified editing form.

Printed by Books on Demand GmbH, Norderstedt / Germany